Steam, Steel & Splendour

Steam, Steel & Splendour

Text by Dave Leitch

HarperCollins*Publishers New Zealand*

First published 1994

HarperCollins*Publishers (New Zealand) Limited*
P.O. Box 1, Auckland

ISBN 1 86950 141 1

Photos as individually credited
Typesetting by IPL Publishing Services, Wellington
Maps by IPL Publishing Services
Design and layout by Geoffrey B. Churchman
Printed in Hong Kong

Half-title page photo: A classic New Zealand railway image of the past - with the Southern Alps in the distance, KB 970 thunders up Cass Bank on the Midland Line with eastbound tonnage for Christchurch on 18 August 1962. J.M. CREBER

Title page photo: Photographed from a tree top, two KAs start train J31 south out of the loop at Raurimu on 19 March 1964. PETER J. MELLOR

Above: This is the stuff that nostalgia is made from - a KA with a 638 express in full flight northbound between Paekakariki and Paraparaumu on 24 October 1960. J.M. CREBER

Page 6: WE 375 heads up the Rewanui Incline with a mixed train in March 1969. J.M. CREBER

Contents

Preface

This book takes a journey back in time to the 1950s and 1960s, a period that many readers probably regard as "the good old days". Although some technologically refined comforts of today were absent, so too was much of the present-day malaise: times were prosperous, unemployment and its concomitant crime were virtually nil, social services functioned properly, there was a general *joie de vivre*, and, of course, for rail enthusiasts, steam was still prominent.

A social service was in many respects how the state railways in this period were regarded. They were run by a government department, and although the National Party, which governed during most of this period, was less enthusiastic about the "social service" concept than the parliamentary opposition and, with a few exceptions, built no new railway lines, trains continued to be run over existing lines until the public clearly demonstrated that it was no longer interested in using them. On the other hand, it could be argued that today's market-driven entrepreneurship, to mould service offerings to what the public actually wanted, was what was needed.

But enough of politics. This book is conceived as a celebration of the last years of steam operation on New Zealand railways, between 1955, when diesels first made a significant appearance, and 1971, when the final demise of steam occurred. While there have been other books on this theme, the use of colour photographs throughout is a first, and adds that extra dimension to give the reader a fuller appreciation of the ways things were.

As the title suggests, the emphasis is on "action" scenes in the picturesque and often spectacular landscapes that New Zealand's terrain provides. In keeping with the usual convention, the progression is a geographic one from north to south. Not every line, depot and locomotive class in use in this period is covered, but there is nevertheless comprehensive representation of them. Most photos are of "genuine article" workings, but a handful of fan trips, early diesel and curiosity scenes are included for completeness.

This book would not have been possible without the contributions of the photographers, particularly John Creber of Auckland, Peter Mellor of Rotorua and Bob Hepburn of Opotiki, to whom all gratitude is expressed.

Geoffrey B. Churchman
Art Director

N

Picton
NELSON
BLENHEIM
Seddonville
Ngakawau
Glen Hope
WESTPORT
Conns Creek
Gowanbridge
Omau
Denniston

Black
-ball
Roa
Ngahere
Rapahoe
Rewanui
GREYMOUTH
Stillwater

Waiau

HOKITIKA
Otira

Ross
Waikari
Arthur's Pass
Waipara

Oxford
Rangiora
Kaiapoi
Sheffield
Darfield
CHRISTCHURCH
White Cliffs
Rolleston
Methven
Little River
Springburn
Southbridge
Mt Somers
Rakaia
ASHBURTON

Pleasant
Point
Fairlie
TIMARU

Hakataramea
Kurow
Waimate
Ngapara
Studholme
Tokarahi
OAMARU

Cromwell
Dunback
Clyde
Makaraeo
Kingston
Palmerston

Roxburgh
Wingatui
Mossburn
Waikaia
Edievale
DUNEDIN
Lumsden
Outram
Waikaka
Ocean Beach
Wairio
Tapanui
Orawia
Hedge
Balclutha
Tuatapere
-hope
Gore
Lovells Flat
Kaitangata
Wyndham
Owaka
Glenham
INVERCARGILL
Tahakopa
Bluff
Tokanui

— — — Closed before 1952

Riding the last steamers

In some ways, steam power today is as vibrant and alive as ever it was. The steaming horses of steel are in lesser numbers now, but scarcity in itself is an attraction in this area, as in any other. So it is that many hundreds of people pay large sums of money for the pleasure of experiencing travel in the discomfort of old suburban passenger cars because they are being hauled by a steam locomotive. They could, if they wished, and for less money, be travelling in great comfort over the same route in one of New Zealand Rail's modern, even luxurious trains.

Yet people cheerfully pay up to ride in old carriages at slower speeds behind a locomotive that, if they are not careful, will put smuts in their eyes.

So why is there this facination with steam? Steam, after all, for the general public, is now an artificial thing, however intrinsically splendid it may still be. The average person in the street today sees the steam locomotive only as a performer - something which is brought out on special occasions to strut its stuff for an adoring multitude of fans, admirers and interested passers-by of all ages and walks of life. It should be noted that this is not the males-only environment it once may have been. Whole families now put up with discomforts that they have paid large sums to experience.

Nostalgia is a wonderful thing; but the world of the steam railway was not that of today's beautifully restored and pampered stars of the steam excursion. The restorers of the locomotives in service today have performed, and are performing, truly amazing feats of resurrection and restoration. They deserve the highest accolades.

But the everyday world of working New Zealand Government Railways steam as it was did not bear a great deal of resemblance to the world of today's restored steam - for which many old railwaymen will echo a fervent "Thank God for that!"

Today at Kingston in the tourist season, a beautifully polished AB class locomotive stands sparkling in the sunshine, shimmering black boiler gleaming with polished brass bands. Steam drifts lazily from the open snifter valves

as the fireman carefully wipes oil off the white painted tyres. In the cab, driver Russell Glendinning casts a glance over the gleaming brass work of the polished boiler backhead and rummages in his bag for the brasso to give a last touch to his glistening charge. The excited chatter of travellers in several tongues and accents makes it very clear that this train is different.

Today's "Kingston Flyer" is a beautiful example of one of the best tourist trains in the country, but it is not, and does not pretend to be, representative of what steam on the NZR used to be about - at least not in the era that I remember best.

As I watched AB 778 awaiting departure recently, I cast my mind back to steam on the Kingston line as I remembered it - rough and ready, hard-working ABs, battered rakes of LA and J wagons loaded with wool, sheep, timber, fertiliser and everything else, including sometimes, no doubt, the kitchen sink. The Kingston line was originally the route to the gold fields, though the gold traffic had long disappeared when I got to know the line in the swan-song days of steam.

Eddie and "Bugs", the branch crew, were old friends from previous trips when, at their invitation, I spent a week on the branch when Southland was still almost 100 percent steam. Even the Invercargill yard shunts at the time were still provided by WW and BB class steam locos.

This time I arrived at Lumsden in great style. The trip down as far as Gore on the express had been largely uneventful, which had perhaps lulled me into complacency. We were late arriving at Gore and I was the only passenger with a ticket for the bus from Gore to Lumsden. The Road Services driver looked at me, at his watch, decided I could be trusted and said, "I'm due at the school committee meeting in half an hour. What d'ya reckon? D'ya mind?"

I said I was game, not wishing to be subsequently reported to Eddie as "Ya bloody mate who made us late the other night". Fortunately the terrain was flat, the bus was empty and there were no delays for minor irritants such as parcels traffic. A Bedford bus of the older variety was, in the hands of a driver late for a meeting, over the Waimea Plains, capable of sustaining nearly 70 mph (113 km/h), though as a passenger I would not describe it as an easy speed! That trip cured any lingering notions I may have had of wanting to be a rally driver. Quite simply, I have "been there, done that"! And when (even as a passenger) you loose your rear on a bend in a Bedford bus, believe me, you know you have lost something! Fortunately the rest of the trip was not at such a furious pace.

Train departure the next morning from Lumsden saw 301 tons tugging on the drawbar (440 tons was the load for an AB up to Eyre Creek). A thinning Scotch mist allowed the occasional spot of sunlight to highlight the specks of soot and the coal dust in which AB 730 was liberally covered, as she wheeled out of town. AB 810 chuffed past on the loop with goods from Mossburn, and we exchanged ribald comments with her crew. The willows along the Oreti River were just changing to autumn gold, the air was fresh, and 730 was in great heart as she took the bit in her teeth and thundered along with the echoes of her exhaust reverberating amongst the willows. The odd pinch of 1 in 84 gradient up to Five Rivers had her grunting a bit, but a pause to shunt off a couple of wagons of "super" gave everyone, including 730, time for a breather.

At Athol, which at that time still sported its chapel (non-denominational) - alias the local surfaceman's hut - there was another shunt and time to pass the time of day with the "cockie" loading out and who, true to form, was bemoaning the weather. At that point there began one of those "incidents" which in part gave rise to the legends which grew up around country branches in the days of steam.

A battered car roared up with a load of enthusiasts out for a day's train chasing, who promptly invited us to "crack a jar" they had brought along for, no doubt, "medicinal purposes". By now, the sun was shining warmly through the golden autumn leaves and the notion of a cool drink was enthusiastically received by one and all.

At Garston the enthusiasts' flagon was empty

On the now closed section of the Kingston Branch, AB 795 leads the Kingston Flyer southbound into Garston in April 1972, not long after the reintroduction of the train. J.M. CREBER

Winter working conditions on the Kingston Branch. A blanket of snow covers the landscape while an AB shunts at Parawa in August 1960. PETER J. MELLOR

and it seemed only reasonable that I should chip in to keep the enthusiast end up. This action was well received by workers and chasers alike. At Kingston there was about an hour's shunting, after which it seemed only neighbourly to accept the enthusiasts' invitation to join them in the bar. We met up with some trampers and soon the afternoon was becoming positively jolly, when it was suddenly noted to be past the hour, meaning we should have been on our way.

As we took slack, there was a sudden shout. "Hey Mister, got room for us?"

Eddie looked round to see two rather attractive young women climbing into the cab.

"How about a lift down the line? I've never been in one of these things." Her accent left no doubt that she hailed from across the Tasman. The two bottles of beer that she was clutching backed up her request. Eddie, whatever else he may have thought about young women and their place in society in general, and on the footplates of railway locomotives in particular, was not known as a man ever to turn down the offer of a free beer.

So it was that we set off up the two miles (3.2 km) of 1 in 62 to 1 in 76 gradient that commenced the climb out of Kingston. The AB rocking and swaying, Eddie linking up the cut-off lever as fast as he dared, Bugs and I taking turns on the shovel, while the exhaust crashed around the glacial deposits and echoed off the far mountain peaks. With a crew of three, two girls and one of the railway enthusiasts in the cab, it was quite a bruising ride as 730 bounced all of us around. We were bucking over the light rail at something approaching 50 mph (80 km/h), the light train of a few empty wagons and the van clattering along in the rear.

At Garston, we again had to stop for a shunt to pick up several JC wagons of sheep which had been loaded after we had dropped the wagons off on the morning run. The Garston pub lost no time in welcoming our passengers, and once again the crew and I decided that it would be a little short of churlish to refuse the generous hospitality that was being offered. Like all good parties, it was warming up noticeably as it went along. By the time we left Garston, we had gained in the cab another enthusiast and the brakeman's wife. With eight aboard it was decidedly crowded when it came time to put on a fire. There was some spirited running, dampened eventually only by the brakeman's insistence that his wife repair to the van and behave herself. With enthusiasts setting the points and amateurs firing, a general air of bonhomie was evident.

Just how evident was revealed when we arrived back (still late) at Lumsden to be faced by the righteous wrath of the District Traffic Manager. That worthy, who had decided that day to take a drive up the line to see how the troops were doing and perhaps even to offer inspiring words to the workers, was suddenly struck speechless. Around the bend in the track, before his astonished eyes, came not a well-ordered goods train laden with the produce of a fertile district, but an AB travelling too fast and loaded to the gunwales with civilians, extra crew and, worst of all, women! And women waving bottles of beer at him no less! He all but drove his car into a roadside ditch. The subsequent bawling-out when he eventually caught up with us, somewhere much farther down the line, was impressive and, as might be expected, the "extras" vanished like mist before the heat of the D.T.M.'s wrath. It seemed we had also missed doing a shunt on the way home. No one had stopped to check whether a wagon derailed on the way up might actually have been rerailed for us during the day.

To add a final note of ignominy to the whole sorry performance, the guard, who was up from Invercargill, had gone to sleep on the way home and missed every shunt from Lumsden to town. He finally woke as his van was being shunted off in the Invercargill yards. It was not one of the more notable demonstrations of NZR efficiency, but it became a talking point in the pubs, on the trains and in the railway yards for days afterwards. It was not untypical of the out-of-sight, out-of-mind philosophy, cheerful errors and bonhomie that were a feature of many a country branch in the good old "steam and 40 mile limit" days.

After that introduction to life on the Southland branches, it seemed very early indeed at 5 am the next day when the alarm rang to get us out for the run to Mossburn with train 627.

This goods had left town at 2.15 am and arrived at Lumsden, if it was on time, at 4.55 am. Eddie and Bugs were due to sign on at 6 am to take the train to Mossburn and return. This task was allowed (including shunts) some 3½ hours for the 21 mile (34 km) return trip. Even then, long before "Rogernomics", one had to wonder at the economics of the exercise. Although a return trip from Invercargill would have been outside the hours allowed one crew, there were three crews rostered for a 122 mile (196 km) round trip to Mossburn. Perhaps not surprisingly, this was when the provision of work rather than efficiency of operation, was what gave New Zealand a then proud record of having no unemployment. Twenty-five or so years later it is not hard to see why the Holyoake years are regarded as golden ones and New Zealand then as the working man's paradise.

Unlike that experienced on the road to Mandalay, dawn was a very quiet affair. The silence of the sleeping town was broken only by the soft exhaust of the AB and (internally at least!) the hammering inside the heads of her crew as we slipped out of town in near pitch darkness. The points were set for the Mararoa Junction, the rather grand name for the set of points at the divergence of the two lines. Curiously, in the Working Timetable at this time, the track to the junction was joint, the Mossburn and Kingston lines both measuring their mileages from Lumsden. Wheels rumbled with a hollow sound as we crossed the decking of the delightful little wooden truss combined bridge over the Oreti River. We rumbled off along the first of the long straights characteristic of the Mossburn Branch proper. Castle Rock, disappointingly nothing more than a standard shelter shed and crossing loop, slipped slowly by, Bugs busy with the shovel in deference to the continuous gradient of the branch.

The glow of the fire flickered around the cab in a baleful orange light as Bugs swung the door open and shut periodically in time with the rhythm of his swings with the shovel. Flickering shadows danced and swayed while the pink sky of dawn turned to grey and the world slowly awoke. What had been a primeval dragon, breathing fire and vapour, rushing through the darkness on some mysterious errand, turned out to be a rather grubby AB class steam locomotive, ageing and battered, that was slogging its way up a country branchline.

The rumble of wheels over a level crossing mingled with the sharper rumble of a constantly working injector. The line had only four gentle curves in the 16 km from the combined bridge to the Mossburn "home" signal, set permanently at "stop". A ringing whistle blast brought the station agent tumbling out to give us the "all clear" with a green flag. We trundled into the yard, which complete with TR shunter and some new yard roads, was clearly reaping the benefit of material coming in for the Manapouri power scheme.

Eddie, as befitted his seniority and probably the severity of his hangover, went off to discuss matters with the Station Master, leaving Bugs and me to do the shunt. For an hour we shunted to and fro, kicking wagons off and placing them around the yard as directed by the signals of the shunter. For me it was a thoroughly enjoyable experience, watching for signals on my side, stoking the fire, working the injector and keeping an eye out for anything else that was going. It was an hour of quite strenuous activity, and a cuppa at the end was welcome indeed.

At 8.40 am we left on the leisurely downhill run back home. Because we were 23 crossing total, we had to stop at the west end of the Oreti combined bridge and call Lumsden for permission to cross it. The Working Timetable required this of all trains heading to Lumsden that exceeded 21 crossing total. The reason for this requirement was that 21 crossing total was the maximum train length that could be stopped short of fouling the points of the Kingston line without leaving part of the train stationary on the bridge.

We sat for some minutes while Ray, our guard, trudged up to the public telephone on the end of the bridge and called the Lumsden Station Master for permission to proceed. Had we been under the 21 crossing total, this little chore could have been done from the railway phone at the junction itself.

At Lumsden we found we were about to pay for the misdemeanours of yesterday, and instead of having the rest of the day off (and being paid a minimum shift allowance) we were to go back up to Five Rivers and uplift the wagons left behind in the revelry of the day before! Running tender first, we set off back to Five Rivers some 10 miles (16 km) up the line. The smoke poured back over the train in a strong headwind with a notable downdraft. Following us on a jigger was "Friendly Fred", the IP Way (Inspector of Permanent Way). It didn't take long for Bugs to see which way the wind was blowing. Judging it to a fine degree, he proceeded to lay on a fire every time the wind was right and poor Fred would disappear in a black sooty cloud!

Long before the arrival of the reinstated Kingston Flyer, tourist buses were a feature of the line, and the half hour we spent shunting and disassembling our train provided great photo opportunities for the tourists, even if we were somewhat less prepossessing than the refurbished Flyer was later to prove.

Next day it was back up the Kingston Branch again, still with fine weather and, like the day before, with AB 726 on the front. There was quite a bit of shunting to do in the Lumsden yard first, but at 11 am we were once again Kingston-bound. The brake pump decided to play up this time and accordingly, at Lowther, Eddie decided he'd better pull the pump apart and see what was what. As a general rule it can be said that there are only two possible breakdowns in the air brake system that make it impossible to proceed - either a compressor failure or a complete failure of the main reservoir system. There are permutations, of course, but it was seldom that a steam locomotive suffered a complete brake failure. Eddie, despite the exhortation in capital letters in item three of the breakdowns section of the manual ("ON NO ACCOUNT SHOULD ANY AIR BRAKE EQUIPMENT BE HAMMERED in an effort to make it work...") simply tried the usual remedy: if it doesn't work, hit it with a hammer. On this occasion, however, the rule book was right and the pump remained obstinately motionless.

Having tested that steam was reaching the governor by loosening one of the steam pipe connections and blowing through, and that the governor was not stuck in the closed position, Eddie had to consider his next move. "When in doubt, lubricate" was always a good steam maxim, and so it proved on this occasion. Eddie, muttering about "lazy bastards" who neglected the fundamentals, took off the main valve chamber covers. Even I could see that it had been a long time since proper lubrication had been effected. Closer examination, however, revealed that congenital laziness was not the problem. Simple grit had blocked the oil delivery feed valve. A generous squirt with the oil syringe soon had things freed up. To our

Above: AB 735 takes water on the Roxburgh Branch on 19 October 1966. In the background is the Clutha River, the damming of which for hydro power north of Roxburgh was the main reason for the continued existence of the branch in the 1960s, as construction materials were hauled there by rail. J.M. CREBER
Below: AB 729 heads a goods train southbound through Fairlight, 14 km south of Kingston, on the Kingston Branch on 9 January 1958. This is now the terminus of the tourist line from Kingston operated by the Kingston Flyer. At the time of writing, proposals were being made to relocate this operation near Queenstown on 7 km of new-built track. BOB HEPBURN

Above: A close-up study of man-made magnificence in harmony with nature: KB 969 hauls no. 150 goods across the Waimakariri River bridge on 29 August 1963. In the background are peaks of the Polar Range. J.M. CREBER

Below: Photographed at Auckland locomotive depot one Sunday afternoon in late 1965 are, from left: KA 947, JA 1276 and JA 1275. J.M. CREBER

combined relief the busy thump, thump, thump of the air pump was once again beating merrily away. It was not quite the end of the problem, though, and on the 1 in 62 downgrade of Eyre Creek there were some heart-stopping moments when the pump suddenly packed up again. Fortunately we were near the bottom of the gradient and had sufficient air in reserve to effect a halt as the downgrade eased into the climb out of Parawa.

Fortunately that, too, seemed to be the last of the grit and we had no further problems. A helter-skelter race with a tourist bus over to Fairlight, before the revived Flyer made such things more commonplace, provided some 45 mph (73 km/h) running and some excitement for tourists and crew alike. Tied up at the wharf awaiting our arrival was the *Earnslaw*, waiting to pick up the contents of two box wagons, having previously loaded coal we had brought up two days before. (Both the Flyer and the *Earnslaw* are still at the lake, though nowadays seldom together at the same time. Both look far more resplendent now as tourist attractions than when they were both merely common workaday objects.)

Shunting completed, 726 clanked off down to the loco depot area to be serviced. Bugs set to work cleaning the fire, pushing a good bank of clinker-free coal up under the brick arch of the firebox and then, by means of the hinged dropgrate, dropping the ash and clinker resulting from efforts with the long fire rake into the ash pit. The heap-up under the brick arch was then spread over the fire bars and fresh coal was applied to give a clean burning fire ready for the run home. Eddie pottered around with the lubricating oil while I filled 726's tender with water. By universal unspoken agreement, only a brew of tea in the guard's van slaked our thirst. By 4 pm, with 12 total in tow, we were on our way back to Lumsden. It is hard to credit today, when the tourist vestige is all that remains of a railway at Kingston, that once Yankee Ks, UBs, Qs, As and ABs, as well as DJ diesels wheeled trains into Lumsden from the four points of the compass. Even on this trip we had shunts at almost every one of the nine stations and halts between Kingston and Lumsden. Overregulated the economy may certainly have been, but it did make for full employment, a very busy railway and a much more closely settled rural landscape than exists today.

As we started on the initial steep gradient, the slog up to Eyre Creek on which we had come within an ace of running away in the morning, Eddie stretched and indicated his seat. "Have a go, Dave".

As the gradient steepened, the old girl began to lose way and I quickly dropped her back a couple of notches on the reversing lever (which in the most simple terms can be compared to a gear lever) and opened up on the throttle. She bellowed satisfyingly and got back into stride. Soon the gradient steepened again, and gravity and tonnage once more tugged her speed down. At the foot of the steep two miles of 1 in 62 she hit a tight 15 chain (300 metre) radius curve, deliberately placed, one could almost suppose, just to introduce a little more challenge into the course. I gave 726 a little more "fat", only to have her decide to lose her footing. As the wheels spun, the exhaust bellowed madly for an instant. By this time both Bugs and I were on our feet, he busy feeding coal into the maw of the roaring fire box, I hovering anxiously ready to grab her if she lost her feet again. The solid hammering beat echoed around the hills as 726 settled into a steady thunderous exhaust beat. We had 300 tons behind on a gradient rated for 330, so we were within two or three wagons of a full load for an AB. It may well have been primitive, unscientific, unsophisticated, inefficient - but by God, it sure got the adrenalin flowing!

While bowling down to Lowther in the gathering twilight, there came an unexpected emergency when a flock of sheep suddenly appeared smack in the middle of the track as we came around a bend. Air blasted from the brake stand as the handle went into emergency, and the brakes grabbed and locked. Rocking and shuddering, we ground to a halt while the sheep parted like the Red Sea. Luckily for the farmer, a few bruises seemed to be the extent of the damage to his flock, and luckily for us, nothing had derailed or bent. We whistled into Lumsden with the self-righteous glow of those who had done a good day's work and, like the Salvation Army, yielded not unto the demon drink!

Next day was Friday and another early start for Mossburn with AB 730, with 420 tons and greasy rail making us work every foot of the way. Drizzle, mist and rain of the kind that every North Islander thinks is the perpetual weather pattern in Southland, was making 730

raise the echoes as she slipped and slid. At Mossburn, Eddie gave Bugs and me a cheerful wave and said, "She's all yours, you two", before disappearing into the warmth of the Station Master's office. The shunt was a heavy one, calling for a lot of punching off of wagons and flying shunts. This is a spectacular manoeuvre, the engine being in front of the wagon being shunted. The shunter has to signal to the driver to slow, lift the coupling hook as the wagons bunch, and signal for rapid acceleration while his mate on the ground has to change the points after the engine has passed and before the wagon arrives at the points! It is exciting, sometimes dangerous for the shunters and/or destructive of wagons, and certainly makes massive steam demands. I rapidly found the AB was using every pound of steam she could get, and Bugs was too fully occupied to spare a glance at the fire, relying on me to see that he got steam. I rapidly learned the truth of two old adages: "The fireman makes the steam and the driver uses it" and "Pressure gauge: the fireman's enemy".

Shunt work makes large and sudden demands for steam, and no sooner, it seemed, did I get the needle heading right the way round the dial, than Bugs would heave on the regulator, 730 would erupt into action and the needle would once again head back down!

In addition, the fireman has to watch for shunt signals on his side of the engine. In my case I had first to learn them! The first day on the shunt I had simply repeated the actual signal the shunter was making, and Bugs had had to provide his own translation. However, a quick course that night had worked wonders and this time I was able to call, "That'll do", "Ease up", "Go out on the side chains", etc. as appropriate.

It didn't take too long, either, to realise that aiming for the bright spots and firing little and often was the way to keep the water hot. After two hours of solid punching and placing of wagons all over the yard, I decided that I had passed my literal baptism of fire. I was a fireman in fact as well as in ambition. Since that time, over 25 years ago, I have long since gained my full locomotive and traction engine-driver's certificates, but I still regard that final test on AB 730 as the day I could first truly say I was a fireman.

After that, the run back to Lumsden where Bugs was due to leave for his holidays, was anticlimactic. A new man had been sent up from town to replace Bugs, and I stayed on the engine with him while Eddie went off to sort out some details with Bugs before the latter departed. The shunter came over and asked us if we would sort out some wagons in the yard for him. As was traditional, the new man, when he got on the engine, looked at the fire and thanked Bugs for having it in good shape. Bugs cheerfully told him it was my fire. It was then a vote of confidence for me when the new man agreed he would do the shunt with me as his fireman.

So once again it was put, place, kick off, accelerate away, stop, go, shovel coal, inject water, watch for the shunter's signals, as the train was torn apart and reassembled. Wagons went to sidings and backshunts, and empties were picked up and placed in order in the train. It was heavy work and in contrast to some later spells in the same yard on DJ class diesels.

Then it was time to take station as assisting engine to AB 729 on a double-header down to Invercargill. The drivers had decided that they would run the lead engine while the firemen ran the second. The regular fireman announced he would go back to the van and sleep and the new man and I would run the second engine. This was promotion indeed - out on the main line in sole charge of the left side!

However, Eddie unwittingly dashed that by saying, "I suppose you blokes will play cards all the way to town?" This idea hadn't occurred to them, so it was a three man crew, me acting but not entirely unsupervised as fireman, that set off on the second engine of this goods to Invercargill. With only 317 tons on the drawbars, the second engine was only for balancing purposes, not muscle, but it made an impressive sight, no doubt.

Steady drizzle was falling as we slowed and then stopped beside a field of turnips. Like a well-drilled military squad, two figures shot out, pulled vigorously, heaved up and swung aboard again. As we spun our wheels on greasy rail, half a dozen fat turnips reposed in muddy splendour on the floor of 729.

There was a shunt at Centre Bush, then as we progressed south, the mist and rain really set in. At Winton I joined the two drivers on the lead engine. The card game in which the firemen were engrossed (surfacing only to keep a quick eye on things) was way beyond my

Above: On its last delivery trip from Greymouth to its resting place at the Te Awamutu Steam Museum, A 423 is seen with its train of enthusiasts at Aickens on the western side of the Southern Alps, some 8 km from Otira, on 29 August 1970. This trip to Christchurch took place in brilliantly clear weather; the day before and the day after were marked by torrential downpours. J.M. CREBER

Below: A KB 4-8-4 heavyweight makes its way up Cass Bank on the eastern side of the Southern Alps with a goods train in August 1963. The first few wagons in the train consist are LA type, laden with timber which overhangs the back ends. PETER J. MELLOR

Above: Smoke trails to Rewanui: after the removal of the centre rail on the incline in 1966, locomotives with unmodified cowcatchers made the journey up the western side of the Paparoa Range. Here Ww 480 climbs between Dunollie and Rewanui in September 1968.

Left: Ww 669 moves a work train between Cronadun and Inangahua on the main line from Greymouth to Westport, on 14 November 1966.
J.M. CREBER

ability to follow. Generally the line was on a mainly gentle downgrade all the way to town, but there were a couple of little pinches running counter to the general flow, and on the short grade out of Lochiel the drivers decided to have a little fun. We started into the gradient and the exhaust notes deepened. The drivers decided it was time to make their mates on the back engine do some work, having correctly guessed without advice from me that a card school would be in progress. The driver in charge of 729 shut his regulator silently, and the sounds of two hard working engines were replaced by the beat of 730 labouring away behind us. She was now pulling over 300 tons and pushing the 87 tons of AB 729.

She was doing famously though, and the clouds of black smoke boiling from her funnel were ample evidence that the card school had long since broken up. The two drivers were just a little put out that the lads were doing so well and decided to introduce a little more challenge to the proceedings. Up came the tender connection cover and down onto the rails went a couple of pints of lubricating oil. The effect, even if expected, was nonetheless startling! Behind us, the hard-working exhaust of 730 suddenly went haywire. The wheels could be heard slipping from our engine. The exhaust shut off, picked up, slipped, caught again, slipped, then, as more oil went down, suddenly went wild again. The firemen then caught on, and the drivers had to open up 729 again before the whole train stalled. There was something about steam working that seemed to encourage camaraderie and the odd bit of horseplay!

An indication of the extent of traffic in pre-deregulation and steam days was a three-way meet on CTC controlled track, overtaking a train off the Wairio Branch, before going into the loop to allow a northbound train to pass. Soon we were heading into the yards, where we dropped off the train and trundled down to the then almost brand-new Invercargill steam shed.

Invercargill was then a wonderful hive of steam activity, almost impossible to imagine in today's truncated railway environment. In 1968 there were still lines to Tuatapere, Wairio, Browns, Bluff, Wyndham, Mossburn, Kingston and Riversdale. Those to Waikaia, Waikaka and Seaward Bush were not long closed. Centralised Traffic Control controlled the busy section to Makarewa. Track still ran further afield to Edievale and Tahakopa. In today's Southland consisting of main line plus Bluff and Wairio Branches, it is difficult to contemplate just what a concentration of railways there was in Southland. And what a concentration of steam it was too! There was almost nothing but steam to be seen. A J took a goods out of Bluff, a WW and a BB handled the yard shunt, A 178, still sporting the fading NZR centennial paint scheme, was on shed. An A stood outside, keeping company with a WF or two, and a J was being serviced for another run.

For a (then) North Islander, the sight of all this steam activity was as welcome as it was unusual, and the WW made no bones about what constituted a smartly handled shunt! Three shunters were kept literally on the run as wagons rattled over points and what seemed like an endless succession of wagons scuttled to and fro, propelled or pushed to their allotted space by the busy little WW.

Then it was time to head down to the main station platform and pick up JA 1263 waiting on the point of train 190, the overnight Friday express to Christchurch. The old familiar heat from an open J class firebox blasted out at me as the hiss of the air-operated doors mingled with the whine of the generator and the rasping scrape of the fireman's shovel as he built his fire for the run ahead. With the needle hovering near the 200 lb (1379 kPa) reading, the whistle shattered the evening air of Invercargill, and while half the city checked its watches, we drew smoothly away with six total in train. With this light train, 50 mph (80 km/h) was reached before we cleared town and the exhaust settled down to a solid staccato roar. I began to think I must have been imagining the speed, but we were through One Tree Point some 5 miles (8 km) from the start with just a fraction over seven minutes on the clock. Invercargill drivers were said to be able to foot it with the best, and I was being served evidence that the stories were no mere rumours. Woodlands at the 11 mile peg (17.6 km) was passed in a fraction over 12 minutes.

In contrast to the ABs, this pace meant bone-jarring, rib-crushing motion. Deafening noise that overrode all else. Smoke rolling down from the funnel, then being whipped away by the slipstream. Hanging on for dear life while adrenalin raged through the veins in dreadful harmony with the thundering steed I was aboard. People chuffing quietly along a tourist railway at 10, 20, 50 km/h, simply have no conception of what it is like sitting apparently in the vent of an active volcano moving at over 100 km/h. It was, quite simply, awe in its most primitive form.

On through the twilight we went, without any diminution of the mad pace. Edendale, the crossing point with the southbound "South Island Limited", came and went at 7 pm but with no sign of the Limited. The signal lights of Gore twinkled in welcome as we swept into the station and changed crews with the late-running Limited. If our run had been exhilarating so far, we lost little pace on the steady rise to Artherton. This four mile (6.4 km) grade never saw speed go below 50-55 mph (80-90 km/h). Such speed on the bank was not favoured by Invercargill crews but it was a trademark of those from Dunedin. For one awful moment I thought speed had overcome gravity as 1263 rolled over into one curve, but centrifugal force was not as I had feared, overcome by momentum and we remained safely on the rails. At the time it seemed to be getting excitingly near the limits of tolerance. Old 1263 heeled into the curve at what seemed like an impossible angle, and had I looked down at that instance, I'm sure the engine would have seemed to be canted over like some crazy cartoon at a kids' matinee. She almost seemed to shake herself as she came back onto even keel again. It still ranks as one of the most exhilarating climbs I have experienced.

At Clinton, the porter came up with the usual welcome cuppa that was the trademark of the Clinton "refresh" (refreshment rooms). Nothing much remains now at Clinton to mark what a major point on the system it once was. It's not even in the railway bible, the Working Timetable. In more civilised (if more uneconomic) times, the porter then proceeded to top up the tender water while the crew relaxed with their sandwiches and the passengers fought for tea and "sammies" or pies. While today's "Southerner" is infinitely more comfortable and convenient, for rail fans it doesn't have that special something of the old days. Even the train number has changed.

It was a busy night on the South Line: we overtook or met several JA-hauled goods as we continued our hectic way north. To be sure, the (one or two) 2,000 tonne trains being hauled daily now on this line make the "little and more often" of steam days look like pups. But then, by their more frequent passage, they made it clear there was a railway in the area - something not so evident now as it once was.

In front, the beam of the headlight silhouetted the outline of the boiler rocking to and fro as the frantic pace continued. The whistle screamed its warning as little country level crossings came and went, the white cross arms reflecting in the headlight beam shining down the track. The soft light from the various gauges on the boiler backhead gave a fitful illumination that was drowned out by the sudden dazzling glare that flooded the cab whenever the firedoors opened. The sweating fireman of 1263 was firing steadily and constantly to keep up with the demand that the speeding express loco was making on its boiler. In a shower of sparks and rolling smoke the black projectile hurtled on through the darkness that surrounded it. There was no mucking about. It was rip, snort and bustle the whole way until we began to slow for the first yard lights of Dunedin. After the pell-mell, hell-for-leather progress, the slowing and smoothness of welded rail near Dunedin was a marked contrast. We drew to a quiet halt at Dunedin's impressive and then much busier railway station.

The fireman slipped down beside the platform edge and lifted the coupling hook to allow 1263 to clank off to "loco" for a well-earned breather. Her replacement JA waited on the loop, steam drifting lazily from the snifter valves, highlighted by the glow of the station lights.

There would be other days and other runs and steam in other forms and places, but these last acquaintances with honest to goodness 100 percent southern steam had been an experience to remember and to cherish. For me, it was never quite the same in the Deep South again.

The South Island was the mecca for New Zealand rail fans as steam in regular services drew to a close. Trains 143 and 144, the "South Island Limited", were regularly chased and photographed as the use of steam diminished and died on the goods trains of the West Coast and the South Island Main Trunk. Perversely, steam made its last stand in New Zealand not on some little branch line goods train, but on the overnight expresses. It was the need for steam heating, an anachronism in itself, that was responsible for the last runs of steam power in main-line scheduled service on NZR. It was on these services that steam saw its final last great hours and demonstrated the unique ability of steam power to give of its designed best, when other forms of motive power would have required an extensive spell in the shops.

It was on JA 1246 one night that I received one of these memorable demonstrations. We had left Christchurch on time, and the usual sedate run through the suburbs gave no indication that this trip would be anything but uneventful. The fireman had been having trouble with the firedoors, and for a moment I had vivid recollections of an earlier heated experience with J 1216 and stuck firedoors, but this time, fortunately, the trouble was in opening, not closing the doors on the raging inferno of the firebox. With manual operation there was no real problem. Investigation showed nothing more than a complete lack of lubrication of the cylinder activating the doors.

"Bloody typical!" roared the fireman. "Too busy pandering to the bloody diesels to do anything for these old girls!" He was obviously a steam man and my heart warmed to his sentiment. A generous squirt with the oil can soon had things right again. By now the cut-off lever was well advanced and the regulator was opened wider as the train began to accelerate through Islington. The long, lonely wail of the whistle echoed for crossings as the lights of the city receded behind us.

It was noticeable that 1246 was not steaming well, and the needle was not much above 160 psi (1100 kPa) as we pounded towards Rolleston while the lights of a long DJ-hauled goods drummed past us on the opposite track. While we waited for "right away" at Rolleston, the fireman set to with the rake, and the fire seemed a better colour when the lights changed and the guard blew departure. Outside the cocoon of the cab, frost glittered in the station lights and the exhaust was a staccato thunder as the wheels slipped on the icy rail of the late autumn night. The engine bucked madly before the sand spurting down onto the rail got the wheels gripping and revolving normally. Another burst of sound erupted along with the driver's cursing before he caught and settled her. Not for nothing was the steam loco called the "iron horse". But as we pulled away, both crew members seemed visibly more at ease with their steed, whose bellowing exhaust echoed in the still air.

The bright green signal lights came and went as the long boiler's silhouette rocked around against the beam of the probing headlight. An increasingly colder breeze whipped around the cab openings. Despite a sack tied between engine and tender on the fireman's side, there was little to cut down the freezing air that crept remorselessly through several layers of clothes. Bankside whistled by at the 30 mile (50 km) peg and at 50 mph (80 km/h). Up to 60 crept the needle as 1246 roared down the bank to the Rakaia River, the crosshead and rods glinting and flashing in the light of a waning moon as they shot back and forth under the pressure of expanding steam. Old fashioned and unsophisticated it may have been, but 400 tons of steel and 200 passengers were moving along at a mile a minute (100 km/h). We took water at Rakaia while the engine was literally enveloped by her own steam in the cold air.

Soon after leaving Rakaia, however, it became noticeable that the pace was slowing.

"What's wrong mate?" yelled the driver to his hapless fireman as the express noticeably lost pressure and momentum. The fireman uttered an unprintable oath and set to with the rake again, rummaging around in the depths of the firebox in a desperate effort to get the needle of the pressure gauge to reverse itself. It was to no avail. Finally and ignominiously, the express was forced to come to a halt out in the middle, it seemed to me, of an empty prairie. As the crashing, banging cacophony of sound ceased, it was possible to get a decent look into the firebox now that the exhaust was shut off. There, looking back at us, was most of the brick arch of the firebox, which had, with the headlong rough-riding progress, finally decided to give up the ghost and fall in on itself, thereby effectively smothering its own fire. A few quick heaves with the rake, and then the offending objects were got out of the way. A ten minute "boil up" and we were once again on our way, a few minutes down but otherwise none the worse for the experience.

The night's fun was not quite over, though. JA 1248, on train 190, should have been crossed at Studholme, but she was also running late and the crossing was not effected until Glenavy, a further 16 miles (26 km) south. When we climbed aboard 1248, she looked in good fettle, and we thought our night's troubles were now over.

We had only gone a few miles when I felt a sharp blow on my foot and fancied I heard the clang of a metal object hitting the floor. With the noise it was impossible to tell. I glanced up and noticed the naked end of the exhaust injector valve, minus its handle. A faint gleam of brass in the corner of the cab by the edge of the boiler backhead betrayed the presence of the offending article which had conveniently wedged itself in the gap between the cab floor and the bottom edge of the firebox. To try to retrieve it was adjudged too risky altogether, so the pump was robbed of its handle, which was placed on the injector.

We then found the light mounted above the exhaust injector drain, situated just behind the trailing driving wheel, was not working. The exhaust injector drain needs to be watched to check whether water is draining out when the handle is turned on. If it is, the injector has not been applied properly and must be shut off and restarted. For the rest of that freezing night, the fireman and I took turns at leaning out of the cab, torch in frozen hand trained on the drain, while the other operated the control handle. It was one small, this time only inconvenient, illustration of the lack of maintenance that at the end greatly increased for the crews the trials of steam operation.

I had more of those trials just two nights later, again on trains 190/189. South of Rakaia, as we went into a dip, the locomotive (JA 1240) gave a twitch as she hit the bottom of the small dip that flung the fireman and me crashing against the window frame in a blow that almost winded us both.

"The old bitch'll either shake herself to pieces or kill us both," shouted the fireman into my ear.

"She's already tried drowning me," I muttered. A few miles back, 1240 had managed to shake loose the clip that held the water pipe to the handle and valve controlling the cab wash-out hose. The attack had been insidious. I had suddenly noticed a wet, cold feeling to my rear and got up to find the water leaking down the inside of the cab wall and forming a pool on the seat on which I was sitting. This and the frosty air had done nothing to make me feel any warmer!

Shortly after leaving Ashburton the tremendous vibration was too much for another part of the equipment. There was the sound of splashing water and the fireman suddenly swung his feet up off the floor.

"The Sellars [the boiler water injector] is falling apart!" he yelled. I looked up, and sure enough the water-feed pipe had detached itself from the Sellars live steam fed, boiler water injector.

"What the hell are you jokers doing?" shouted the driver, very amused from the safety of his (dry) side of the cab. "Trying to sabotage the outfit?"

I held a torch while the fireman did his best to screw up the offending pipe. Getting the pipe back on wasn't hard. Screwing the ring that held it in place on the base of the injector, sufficiently tightly to survive the rollicking gait of 1240, was quite another matter. The ring had to be tapped tight with a hammer and a cold chisel inserted in the notches of the locking ring. The fireman, with his left arm behind the exhaust injector water lever, his hand gripping the chisel and trying to hold it long enough to belt it with the hammer, had an unenviable job. His face was literally a fraction of an inch from the side of the boiler backhead. Even crouched down as I was and able to hang onto the firedoor handle with one hand while I directed the torch with the other, it was bad enough. Eventually the nut was tightened sufficiently and the sweating fireman stood up and stretched his cramped muscles.

"It's not bloody fair," he snarled. "They do stuff all to look after these old girls, but if a diesel breaks down we simply ring for a fitter. On these we're expected to be our own damn fitters!"

The ordeal was not quite over yet, however. A sudden blast of steam and spraying hot water galvanised the crew into action to shut down one of the boiler water level gauges which had suddenly shattered.

"Be lucky if there's a bloody engine left soon," growled the fireman with justifiable ill grace.

At Timaru we fortunately had time to effect repairs properly to the various items of malfunctioning equipment. Apart from bad smoke blow-back all the way, the trip home on J 1236 was without incident. We all felt we'd had enough!

There was, though, an amusing postscript to the evening. As we were walking away from 1236 at Linwood to go to the crew room, a young cleaner spotted us.

J 1235 with a goods train bound for Taneatua makes its way through a shallow cutting between Te Puke and Otamarakau in the Bay of Plenty in September 1965. J.M. CREBER

"Cripes. Look at these dirty bastards," he called to another cleaner.

"Bloody diesel nit," was our driver's only rejoinder. We were all too tired to take much notice of the pointing cleaner. The cause of his mirth soon became apparent, though.

I glanced in the mirror and an unfamiliar black face looked back. I actually turned around to see who it was standing behind me before the realisation struck that it was in fact my face in the mirror. White eyeballs stared at me out of a literally coal-black face, with a shining white forehead when I removed my cap. It was at least twenty minutes of hard scrubbing before I was decent enough to be able to collect the rest of my gear from the station. Black rings around my eyes persisted for two days as a souvenir of an eventful and smokey trip on steam in the dying days of its regularly timetabled use on the NZR.

With the exception of those lovingly preserved star performers of the main line and lesser scale private line operations, the "iron horses" have gone to Pacific Steel's knackers yards. The pall of smoke of a Sunday evening light-up has disappeared from the locomotive depots of the now privately owned New Zealand Rail Ltd. Rather cleaner electrics draw down power for their 3,000 hp developing traction motors. Rebuilt and original-style diesels, coupled in multiple, chant their internal combustion song along today's ribbons of steel.

They all have their own fascination, but for me they will never have the majesty, the primeval, elemental force and obvious, seemingly unlimited power that characterised the steam locomotive in its lusty prime. The thunderous shouting of defiance of grade and gravity. The streaming wisp from the exhaust of a JA charging at over 70 mph across the Canterbury Plains. They were great days!

David Leitch

Section One
The North Island

Railways developed more slowly in the North Island than in the South Island. Before the advent of the "Vogel Era" in 1870, there had been no significant construction in the North Island at all. Even ten years later, the network length in use in the North Island totalled just 600 km, compared to the 1,300 km in the South Island.

To some degree this was due to the greater extent of flat terrain in the South Island, but primarily it was because the population of the South was then much larger. With the gradual drift of population and economic activity to the North, this changed, and by the turn of the century, North Island construction was proceeding at a faster rate than in the South.

Just as construction of the network was slower in the North Island than in the South Island, so too has been its latter day pruning. The net reduction in the North Island network since its peak in the early 1950s has been only 179 route kilometres, with 276 km of line closures being offset by 97 km of new line openings - and the closures included 60 km of the East Coast Main Trunk being made redundant by the Kaimai deviation in 1978. In the South Island there have been over 1600 km of closures in the same period, with no new line openings.

Sir Julius Vogel's vision of a network of trunk lines linking all the major centres gradually saw realisation in the North Island. If one can exclude Kaitaia in the far north, Gisborne was the last provincial centre to receive a rail connection (from the south) in the mid 1940s. Another link for Gisborne north to the East Coast Main Trunk was the only obvious gap in the North Island system that was never closed.

As in the South Island, locomotive power in the early years consisted of small tank locomotives, suitable for lightweight track and tight curves. The first-designed of these, the 0-6-0 saddle tank F class, was the most successful, and with a total of 88 built, was exceeded in numbers only by the 152 of AB class in the 20th century. Generally most locomotive classes were built (and some converted) in small batches - often only in single figures - and soon a great variety appeared on New Zealand rails.

Letters of the alphabet were used to denote different classes (some being used more than once), with a second letter to denote a subclass. Numerals were used to identify each individual member, although these often did not follow a consistent or logical order.

Although New Zealand was then a devoutly British colony, its railway engineers quickly recognised that American locomotive designs were more appropriate for New Zealand conditions. The first tender locomotive was the British built J class (2-6-0). The next, however, was the K class (2-4-2), obtained from the Rogers Locomotive Works of New Jersey, which arrived in 1878. American-supplied locomotives all proved suitable and performed well. The same was not true of every British-designed class. Following a fiasco in the mid 1880s with the V class from Nasymth Wilson & Co., which was well overweight, no more locomotives of British design were imported, although a number of successful locomotives of New Zealand design continued to be built in Britain.

W was the class letter reserved for tank locomotives from the late 1880s onwards, and the first of these, W 192, was the first locomotive built in New Zealand Government Railways workshops in 1889, although earlier an order had been given to Scott Brothers of Christchurch for some of the D class tank locos.

Most classes were originally earmarked for particular lines, but the majority saw use in various parts of both islands. One notable exception, however, and which became internationally famous, were the H class 0-4-2T Fell engines used on the 5 km Rimutaka Incline, in the southern Wairarapa, from 1878. With the opening of the Rimutaka Tunnel in 1955, they and the Rimutaka Incline passed into history.

Contributions to the fleet from private enterprise initiative were few, but a major exception were those of the Wellington and Manawatu Railway Company, which built the line between Wellington and Longburn (just south of Palmerston North). Initially the company obtained its engines from the UK, but from 1888 onwards obtained them from Baldwin of Philadelphia, which builder also supplied a number of NZR classes. The latter included the Q class in 1901, the first class in the world with the 4-6-2 wheel arrangement, known from then on as the "Pacific" type.

With the development of greater motive power needs following the completion of the North Island Main Trunk between Wellington and Auckland in 1908, came the X class, the first class in the world to be designed with the 4-8-2 wheel arrangement, which from 1911 became known as the "Mountain" type, although this term came from locomotives built for the mountainous lines of the Chesapeake & Ohio railroad in the USA.

Further experimentation with increased locomotive power for the North Island led to three Garratt-type articulated locomotives (4-6-2+2-6-4) being built in the late 1920s. These developed the greatest tractive effort of any locomotive in New Zealand (until the EF electrics appeared in 1986). But design faults saw their lifespan limited and within ten years they had been reconstructed into six "Pacifics", although these retained the G classification.

In 1932, just three years after the appearance of the Garratts, came the class that was to be for many people the epitome of NZR: the 4-8-4 Ks.

Like the later J class they attracted a great deal of attention internationally, being more powerful than equivalent standard-gauge British locomotives. They were accordingly described as "quart-sized power on a pint-sized railway". In New Zealand the expression "as strong as a K engine" was common for many years. The 71 members of the K series were used in the North Island, except for six KBs, which were mainly used on the South Island's Midland Line between Springfield and Arthur's Pass.

The final development of New Zealand steam locomotives occurred with the J class. Of the "Mountain" 4-8-2 wheel arrangement, they in some respects resembled a stretched version of the AB - the "maid of all work" of NZR which had first appeared during the First World War. It was intended as a main line express passenger and goods engine, but which could be used on lighter rail than the Ks. The 91 members of the J series were produced between 1939 and 1956 and used in both islands. Some were to see less than 20 years' service.

Steam came to a close earlier in the North Island than it did in the South Island, with some of the J series being transferred south. The last recognised run of a regularly scheduled steam-hauled goods train took place with JB 1213 (a J converted to burn oil rather than coal) on a Bay of Plenty goods train on 17 October 1967.

The last steam-hauled passenger train in the North Island run by NZR was a Christmas special between Frankton and Claudelands in Hamilton on 23 December 1967.

Northland

Above: J 1209 sits at Opua with a no. 50 passenger express for Auckland, waiting for departure, on 7 November 1956. Opua is the terminus of the branch to the scenic Bay of Islands, but which last saw NZR freight traffic in 1985. The Kawakawa to Opua section is now the setting for a seasonal tourist steam railway. J.M. CREBER

Below: WW 556 at the terminus of the Donnelly's Crossing Branch ready to depart with no. 128 goods with passenger car attached, on 9 January 1957. The 36 km line from Dargaville was closed on 19 July 1959 and the loco was withdrawn in 1963. J.M. CREBER

Above: The same train as in the bottom photo opposite, seen between Kaihu and Dargaville.
J.M. CREBER
Below: WW 556 seen again with no. 131 with car goods for Donnelly's Crossing, departing Whatoro.
J.M. CREBER

Above: AB 759 *heads a shunt from Waro to Whangarei on 3 March 1962, seen here approaching Hikurangi.* J.M. CREBER
Below: J 1215 *plus* AB 712 *ready to depart Whangarei with a goods train on 24 May 1962.* J.M. CREBER
Opposite below: Between Waiotira, the junction for the branch to Dargaville, and Waikiekie, AB 712 *is seen with no. 36 mixed train on 8 November 1956.* J.M. CREBER

Above: Ten kilometres to the south of Whangarei at Portland, a DF is seen arriving with no. 102 goods for Auckland on 22 February 1957. The 10 member DF class were the first mainline diesels to appear on NZR (in 1954), and although themselves undistinguished (all being withdrawn early by 1975), they were the portent of things to come. In some people's opinion, the DF was NZR's most photogenic diesel. J.M. CREBER

Right: At the Portland Cement Works, an industrial steam loco, company no. 7 (ex-NZR L 508) is seen on the same day. J.M. CREBER

Above: On 8 November 1956, J 1207 heads no. 73 with car goods at Taipuha. J.M. CREBER
Below: On 28 February 1962, AB 759 heads a shunt out of Whangarei to Waro, 20 km north. J.M. CREBER

Auckland

Above: WAB *796 is seen between Mt Albert and Baldwin Avenue with no. 61 suburban passenger train on 13 January 1958. At the time this was still a single-track section, the line not being duplicated until 1968.* J.M. CREBER

Below: J *1201 on no. 21 goods passes through Croydon Road station in west Auckland on 22 January 1957.* J.M. CREBER

Above: WAB *801 with no. 119 passenger train for Papakura steams up the Parnell bank to Newmarket on 2 March 1957.* J.M. CREBER

Below: Mainline departures from Auckland were more spectacular. Here JA *1275 and* KA *940 head no. 227 express to Wellington out of Auckland station on 14 June 1958.* J.M. CREBER

Above: At Auckland locomotive depot in 1958, power line-ups such as this were standard. Seen here are an AB, a C, a WAB, and a fleet of North British built JAs. PETER J. MELLOR
Below: BB 619 and WW 679 shunt trains at Auckland on 3 June 1957. J.M. CREBER

Above: K 913 heads no. 385 goods for Frankton along the Main Trunk between Meadowbank and Glenn Innes on 14 June 1958. J.M. CREBER
Below: A JA-hauled express 153 to Wellington is seen shortly after 6 pm one Sunday evening early in 1965 between Meadowbank and the Purewa tunnel. J.M. CREBER

Above: WAB *802 on no. 181 suburban passenger train is seen between Panmure and Silvia Park on 14 January 1958.* J.M. CREBER
Below: WAB *800 heads a goods train south near Ellerslie in late 1964 next to a southern motorway that was a lot less busy then than it is now.* J.M. CREBER

Above: Overkill for the train size, perhaps, but J 1206 still makes an impressive sight as it departs Ellerslie with a passenger train for Papakura on 22 April 1957. J.M. CREBER
Below: WAB 801 on no. 123 passenger train for Papakura departs Penrose (junction for the branch line to Onehunga) on 11 April 1957. J.M. CREBER

As these photos indicate, the W<small>AB</small> tank locos were the mainstay of Auckland suburban services. Right: No. 801 on no. 103 suburban passenger train departs Westfield on 19 October 1956. J.M. CREBER

Middle: The same service but a different W<small>AB</small>, no. 764, a kilometre further south at Otahuhu on 26 October 1956. J.M. CREBER

Bottom: Also at Otahuhu, W<small>AB</small> 796 departs with no. 170 passenger train on 16 December 1957. J.M. CREBER

Waikato & Bay of Plenty

Coal mining was the reason for the construction of the 24.1 km branch line from Huntly to Glen Afton between 1915 and 1924. As well as industrial (non-NZR) spurs, it also had connections in the form of 61 cm gauge cable inclines.

Above: BB 635 and a private Peckett locomotive at the Glen Afton terminus in October 1956. THE LATE DEREK CROSS

Left: Another private Peckett takes loads from the collieries to the NZR railhead at Pukemiro in 1957. PETER J. MELLOR

Bottom: F 185, built by Dubs in 1878, was still working for the Mines Department in the 1950s. It is seen here at Rotowaro (the present-day terminus of this line, 8.6 km from Huntly) on 14 October 1957. BOB HEPBURN

Above: BB 635 heads train 278 between Pukemiro and Glen Afton in 1957. PETER J. MELLOR
Below: BB 618 leaves Huntly with a miners' train for Glen Afton in the winter of 1965. J.M. CREBER

Above: At Rotowaro, BB 618 arrives with its Glen Afton train, while a private Hawthorne-Leslie (ex-Ohai mines in Southland) waits for a connection to the Mahons mine. BB 618 was written off the following year. J.M. CREBER
Below: AB 703 heads a loaded coal train between Rotowaro and Mahuta in late 1965. The loco was also written off the next year. J.M. CREBER

The 10.6 km State Mines Department branch from Ngaruawahia (on the NIMT) to its coal mines near Glen Massey, known as both the Wilton Collieries Line and the Glen Massey Branch, was worked by NZR from 1935 until its closure on 19 May 1958.

Above: On 8 July 1957, BB 635 prepares to leave Ngaruawahia with a string of empties for the mine. PETER J. MELLOR

Left: The same train underway to the mines. BB 635 was written off in 1965. J.M. CREBER

Opposite: On 8 July 1957, BB 635 heads a train of empty coal wagons from Ngaruawahia to the terminus of the Wilton Collieries Line. J.M. CREBER

Above: KA 953 heads a passenger train on 9 May 1964 on the North Island Main Trunk between Huntly and Taupiri. J.M. CREBER

Below: Frankton (Hamilton) was a well-known depot in steam days. With the building and opening of the Te Rapa marshalling yard depot in the early 1970s, it closed. BB 171 shunts on 23 August 1957. J.M. CREBER

Above: At the end of the 19.2 km Cambridge branch, the first encountered on the East Coast Main Trunk from Hamilton, BB 65 and AB 715 head train 280 in the early spring of 1956. THE LATE DEREK CROSS
Below: WAB 764 on no. 337 goods for Kinleith passes through Matamata on 7 November 1958. J.M. CREBER

Opposite above: WAB 767 on no. 291 goods seen between Putaruru and Lichfield on the Kinleith Branch on 9 November 1957. J.M. CREBER
Opposite below: K 913 and WAB 767 seen in the same locality in the same year. THE LATE DEREK CROSS

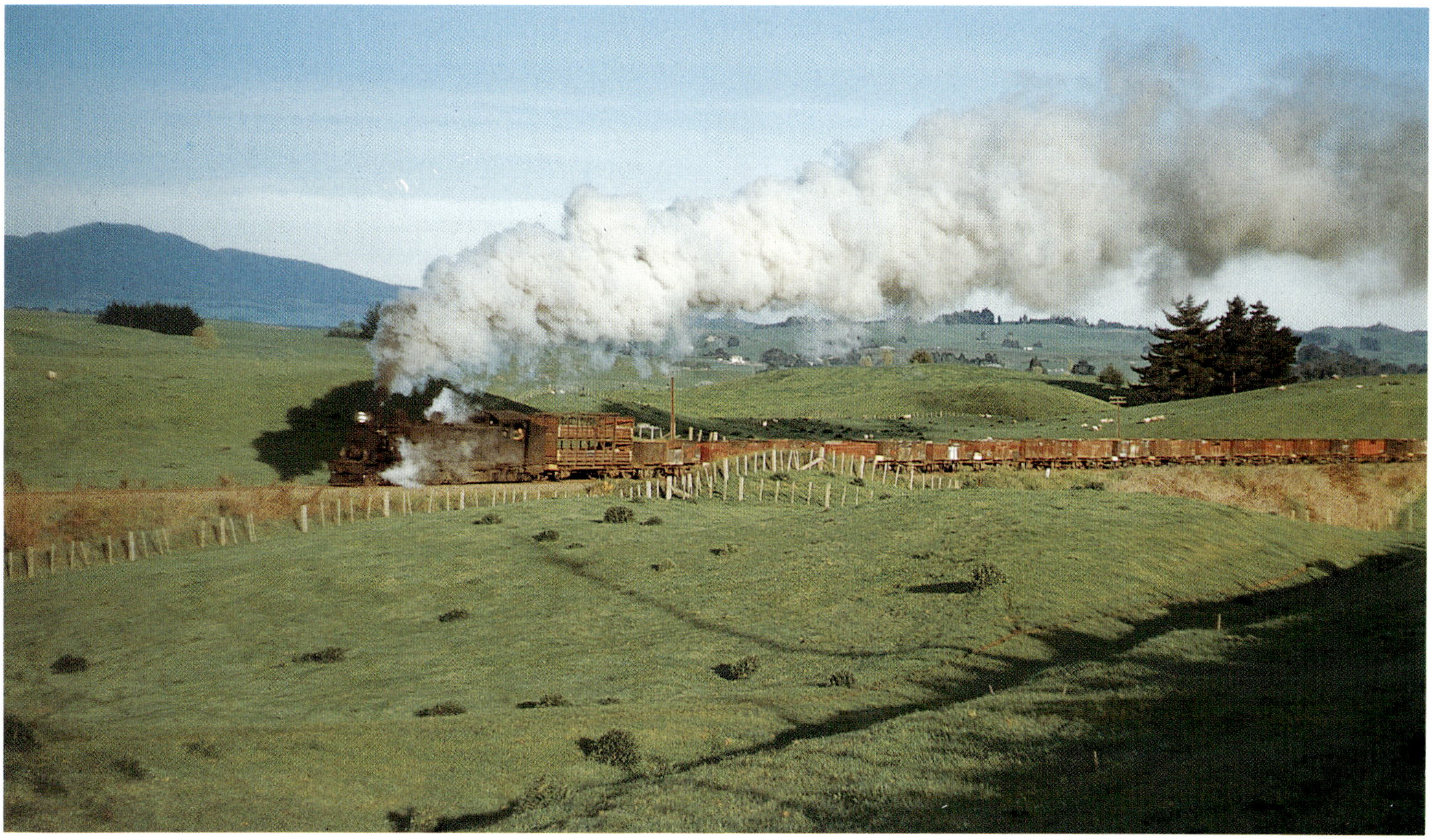

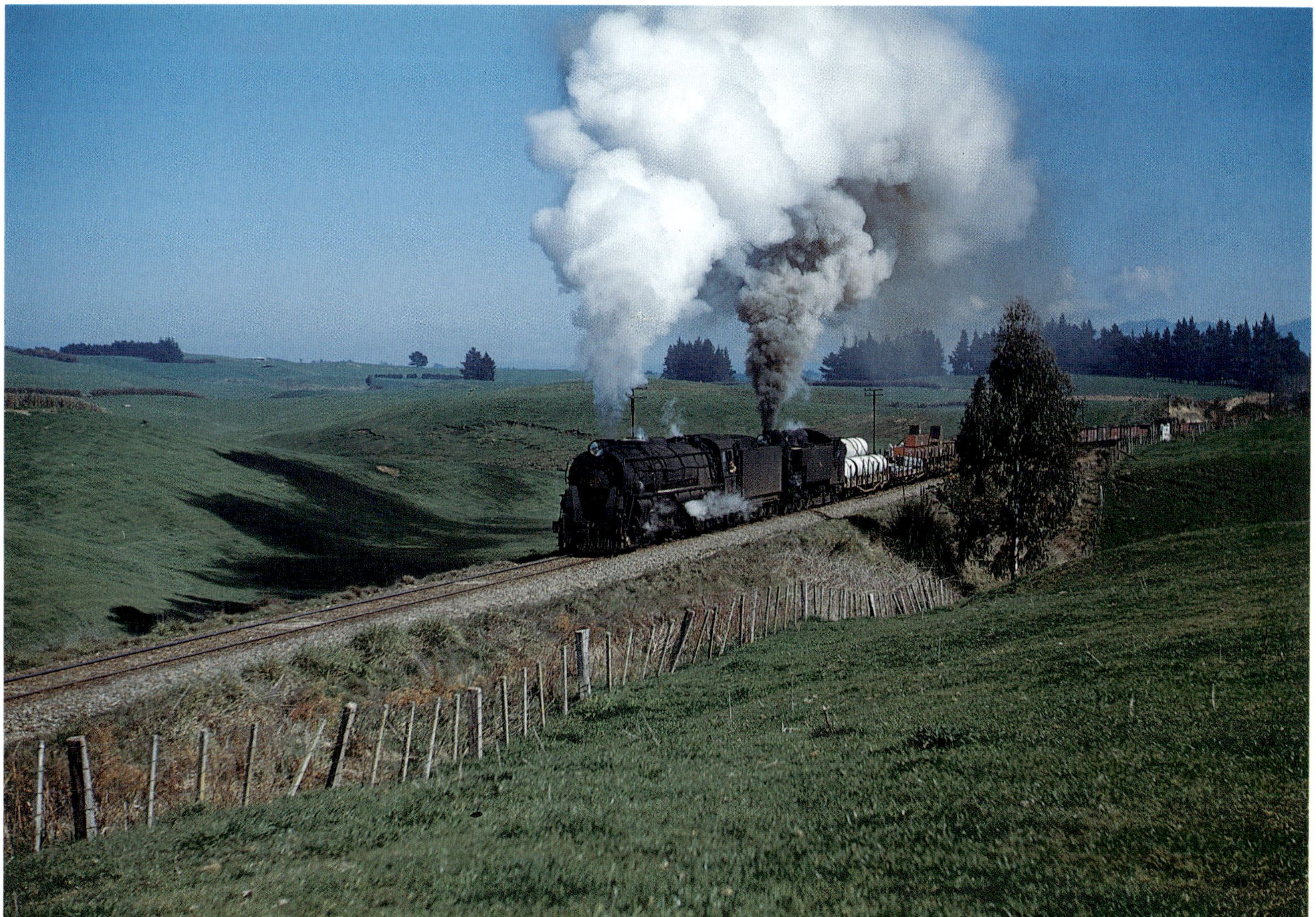

Above: W_AB 687 *with no. 289 goods for Kinleith departs Tokoroa on 6 February 1959.* J.M. CREBER
Below: B_B 144 *on an NZRLS excursion train to Te Aroha heads through the Piako yard on 30 July 1966.* J.M. CREBER

Above: The branch to Rotorua ascends and descends the Mamaku ranges, reaching a maximum altitude of 620 metres. KA 940 heads an excursion train from Rotorua between Ngongataha and Tarukenga on 1 June 1964, with Lake Rotorua in the background. J.M. CREBER

Below: At Mamaku on the Rotorua branch, and near its summit, JA 1281 heads a rather insubstantial train 240, one day in August 1956. THE LATE DEREK CROSS

Above: J 1223 on no. 357 goods, assisted by J 1221, departs Paeroa on 22 November 1958. J.M. CREBER

Left: JA 1285 on no. 121 express for Taneatua arrives at Paeroa on 7 February 1959, the second to last day of this service. With the introduction of the Fiat railcars, rail passenger services beyond Te Puke ended. J.M. CREBER

Above: J 1223 with the Taneatua Express approaches the 1,006 metre long Karangahake Tunnel from the northwestern side on 11 October 1958. J.M. CREBER

Below: J 1225 on no. 322 express for Auckland from Taneatua approaches the southeastern entrance to the tunnel in the Karangahake Gorge on 22 November 1958. J.M. CREBER

Above: J 1223 on no. 357 Tauranga goods between Waikino and Athenree. J.M. CREBER
Below: A J with a mixed train heads between Waihi and Waikino on 11 October 1958. J.M. CREBER

*Above: J*B *1233 heads a goods train through Waihi in 1966.* J.M. CREBER
Below: J 1223 on no. 328 with car goods arrives at Waihi on 22 November 1958. J.M. CREBER

Above: JA 1282 with train 281, a Frankton-Tauranga goods, seen between Waimata and Athenree in 1966.
J.M. CREBER

Left: J 1231 and AB 701 on no. 328 with car goods from Tauranga approach Omokoroa on 29 September 1957.
J.M. CREBER

Above: J 1219 on no. 281 with car goods for Tauranga departs Otumoetai on 2 September 1957. J.M. CREBER
Below: AB 701 with no. 319 with car goods for Taneatua heads along the Tauranga harbour at Strand on 16 September 1957. In the background can be seen Mt Manganui. J.M. CREBER

Above: J 1204, on a goods train from Taneatua, has its water stocks replenished between Awakaponga and Matata on 20 July 1963. J.M. CREBER

Left: A locality with a similar but different name, and also on a railway route, is Matamata. WAB 764 passes through the yard with no. 337 goods for Kinleith on 7 November 1958. J.M. CREBER

Above: *J 1204 with the same train is seen along the coastal section between Matata and Otomarakau. In the background is Motuhora Island.* J.M. CREBER
Below: *At the end of a 14 km private line from Awakeri (on the Taneatua Branch) the Whakatane Board Mills Co. had a yard shunter in the form of ex-NZR FA 41, seen here in 1960.* THE LATE DEREK CROSS

Above: J 1222 waits at the terminus of the Taneatua Branch with express no. 322 for Auckland on 26 September 1958. J.M. CREBER

*Below: The 57 km branch from Kawerau to Murupara, built for logging traffic and handed over to NZR in July 1957, was diesel worked from the outset, like the Wairarapa Line from Wellington once the Rimutaka tunnel was opened at the end of 1955. A pair of D*G *locomotives (like the D*Fs, *a product of English Electric), haul loaded log wagons to Kawerau in August 1957.* THE LATE DEREK CROSS

The King Country

Above: KA 942 and KA 946 thunder along the North Island Main Trunk central section with goods train J31 in tow between Kakahi and Owhango on 22 April 1964. J.M. CREBER
Below: In September 1963, KA 934 drifts down towards Kakahi above the Whakapapa River and across the site of a notorious unstable hillside which frequently caused trouble for the railway. PETER J. MELLOR

Above: KA 934 and KA 943 head a winter snow excursion train on 17 July 1965 between Piriaka and Manunui. J.M. CREBER
Opposite above: KA 950 with M96 goods passes Oio on 23 April 1964. J.M. CREBER

*Below: Two K*As *leave a long trail of exhaust steam hanging in the air as they lift train J31 between Owhango and Oio in May 1964.* PETER J. MELLOR

Above: KA 946 on no. 155 goods heads between Oio and Raurimu on 19 November 1963. J.M. CREBER
Below: A flameout, an artificially induced phenomenon which was even more spectacular at night! KA 945 startles the inhabitants of Raurimu in 1964. PETER J. MELLOR

Above: At the bottom of the famous Raurimu Spiral, northbound KA *948 sits with no. 456 goods awaiting a southbound crossing on 23 April 1964.* J.M. CREBER
Below: In the same location, looking in the opposite direction, the fireman of KA *941 gets his feet wet taking water, while the driver amuses himself making a snowman on the headstock. The crew of* KA *934, the second engine, stay in their cab. Train J31, September 1964.* PETER J. MELLOR

Above: KA 958 ascends the Raurimu Spiral with no. 155 goods on 22 November 1963, with the township of Raurimu in the background. J.M. CREBER
Below: KA 948 and KA 950 with train J31 storm across the Piopiotea River, about halfway between Raurimu and National Park during a severe snowfall on 3 September 1964. PETER J. MELLOR

Above: KA 942 and KA 948 descend the Raurimu Spiral with no. 456 goods on 22 April 1964, with Mt Ngauruhoe in the distance. J.M. CREBER
Below: KA 948 with no. 456 goods arrives at Erua on 23 April 1964. J.M. CREBER

Above: KA 945 crosses the Makatote Viaduct with a southbound goods train early on a morning in December 1963. At 79 metres high, this was the highest viaduct on the North Island Main Trunk until the completion of the Mangaweka-Utiku deviation in the 1980s. PETER J. MELLOR
Below: WAB 687 works the Railway Enthusiasts replica of the 1920s "Daylight Limited" across the Makatote Viaduct in October 1961. PETER J. MELLOR

Above: The addition of a snow blizzard changes the scene as KA 950 crosses the Makatote Viaduct southbound with train J31 in the winter of 1963. PETER J. MELLOR
Below: Not far south of the Makatote Viaduct is the 34 metre high Manganui-o-te-Ao Viaduct, crossed here by KA 950 and northbound goods train 456 after a heavy snowfall in 1964. Not long after, this viaduct was replaced by a new structure. PETER J. MELLOR

Left: Two KAs with goods trains cross at Rangataua in the winter of 1961.
PETER J. MELLOR

Below: KA 946 on no. 155 goods storms up the bank prior to arriving at Waiouru on 19 November 1963. Mt Ruapehu makes a fine backdrop.
J.M. CREBER

Night steam on the "Trunk": Above: KA 934 pauses at Taihape with the Wellington to Auckland Sunday night express no. 628. Below: Express 227 from Auckland pauses at Raurimu for passengers and mail. On the end is a Railway Travelling Post Office van. After these vehicles were withdrawn in 1971, they became buffet cars on the original "Northerner" service and were finally converted into business cars for the railway administrators. PETER J. MELLOR

Above: With Mt Ruapehu in the distance, KA 943 heads on no. 155 goods between Waiouru and Hihitahi on 20 July 1962. J.M. CREBER
Below: JB 1224 on no. 555 goods for Taumarunui has completed its journey over the Stratford-Okahukura line as it approaches the junction at Okahukura on the North Island Main Trunk in July 1961. J.M. CREBER

Taranaki & Wanganui

Above: The line connecting Taranaki directly with the North Island Main Trunk - the Stratford to Okahukura Line (SOL) was one of the last completed in the North Island and traverses impressively wild terrain. JB 1203 on no. 555 with car goods for Taumarunui is seen between Tuhua and Okahukura on 12 October 1963. J.M CREBER

Below: JB 1229 on no. 556 goods for Stratford is seen between Tuhua and Okahukura on the SOL on 12 November 1960. J.M CREBER

Above: WW 561 on an NZRLS excursion heads between Haeo and Ohura on the SOL on 21 October 1961. J.M. CREBER

Below: K 906 arrives at Hawera with a goods train, and crosses tracks to bypass an excursion train standing at the station platform, at the beginning of November 1960. J.M. CREBER

Above: K 912 and K 914 with a passenger train to New Plymouth attack the 1 in 35 gradient of the Westmere Bank out of Aramoho (Wanganui) on 12 March 1962. J.M. CREBER
Below: K 907 and K 912 on an NZRLS excursion between Waitotara and Nukumaru on 30 March 1962. J.M. CREBER

Above: Locomotive Ww 561 is seen again on the main Taranaki line departing Waitotara on 5 November 1960.   J.M. CREBER

Below: AB 708 and AB 819 on an NZRLS excursion to Waitotara from Wanganui are seen near Aramoho in 1965.   J.M. CREBER

Hawkes Bay & Gisborne

Above: On 27 February 1959, one month before the closure of the line, AB 826 works a short ballast train on the 78 km Motouhora branch, along the course of the Motu River. BOB HEPBURN
Below: ABs 736 and 738 head G31 express across the Maraetaha River, south of Muriwai on the Napier-Gisborne line. BOB HEPBURN

Above: JA 1290 heads a southbound goods train between Waikokpu and Nuhaka in November 1965.
J.M. *CREBER*
Below: Near the location of the Blue Slip, JA 1289 heads a southbound goods in the same month. J.M. *CREBER*

Above: The 39 metre high Kopuawhara Viaduct, one of the more striking of the NZR network, is crossed by a JA with a southbound goods train in November 1965. J.M. CREBER
Below: Wairoa in 1965 had a locomotive depot for trains beginning and terminating there. J 1227 and AB 751 are seen awaiting turns of duty. J.M. CREBER

Above: A KA heads G12 express across the Waitangi bridge (Tutaekuri River) north of Clive at Easter 1960. BOB HEPBURN

Below: Amid grassland dried by summer heat, KA 952 climbs the Opapa Bank with P 23 goods, consisting of refridgerated meat wagons on 22 December 1957. BOB HEPBURN

Above: K 909 skirts Opapa Lake at the top of the Opapa Bank on 30 December 1960. BOB HEPBURN
Below: KA 952 on no. 932 goods for Napier departs Hatuma on 6 April 1963. J.M. CREBER

Above: KA 936 crosses the Tukituki River north of Waipukurau with train 932 in October 1965. J.M. CREBER
Below: KA 931 on no. 932 goods at Waipukurau, about halfway between Hastings and Dannevirke, on 3 November 1961. J.M. CREBER

Above: On 7 November 1961, KA 958 on no. 932 goods crosses KA 936 at Waipukurau. J.M. CREBER
Below: J 1227 and AB 838 on no. 932 goods arrive at Kopua, about 30 km south of Waipukurau, on
17 November 1961. J.M. CREBER

Above: Shortly before, the same train as in the photo on the bottom of the previous page, is seen crossing the 39 metre high, curved Ormondville Viaduct. J.M. CREBER

Below: AB 819 on no. 6 shunt arrives at Ormondville on 30 October 1961. The station building is now in the care of a preservation group. J.M. CREBER

Above: KA 963 with no. 915 goods departs Ormondville southbound, with the township in the background, on 28 November 1962. J.M. CREBER
Below: KA 933 on no. 933 goods seen between Matamau and Piripiri on 19 November 1962. J.M. CREBER

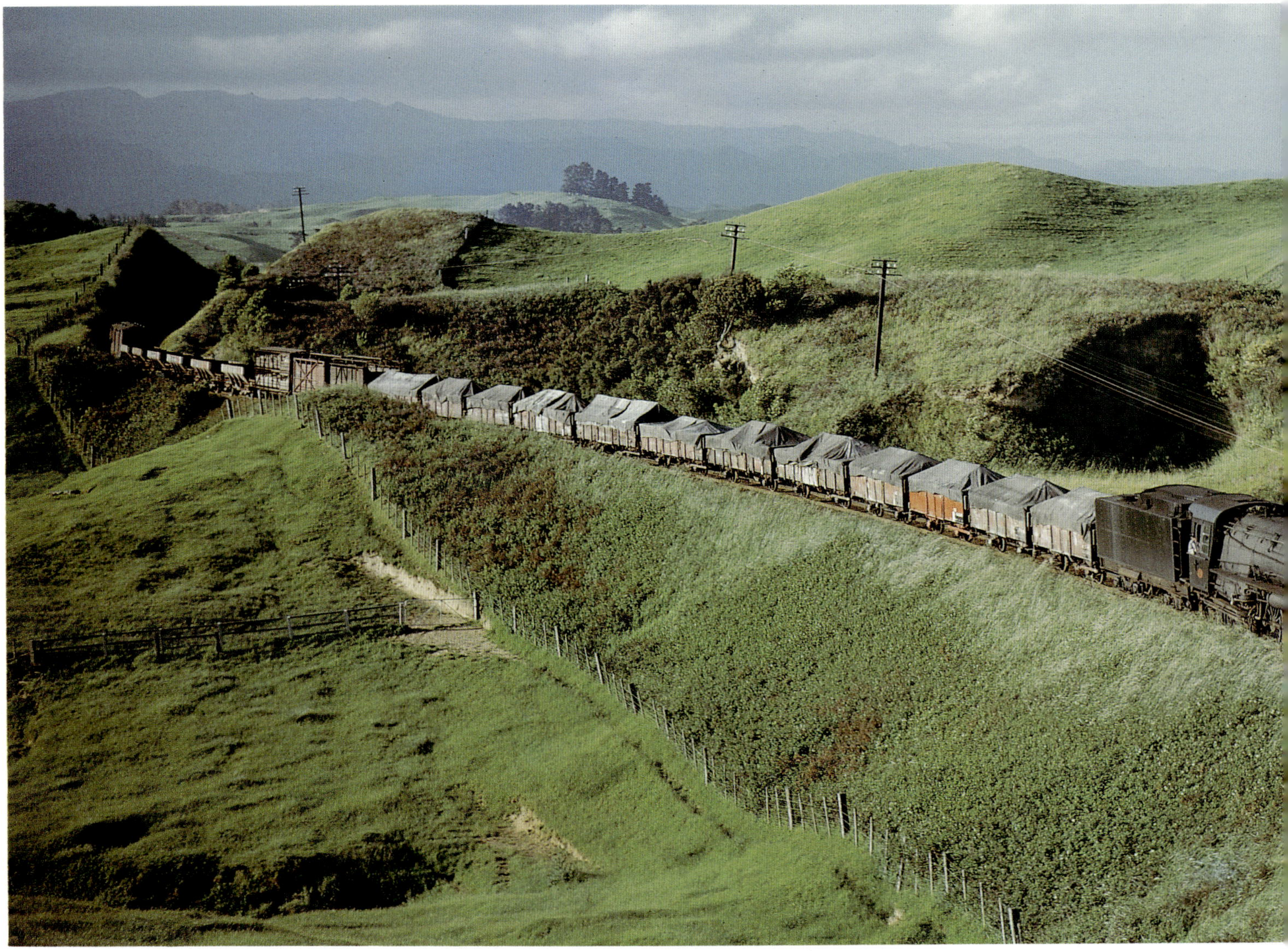

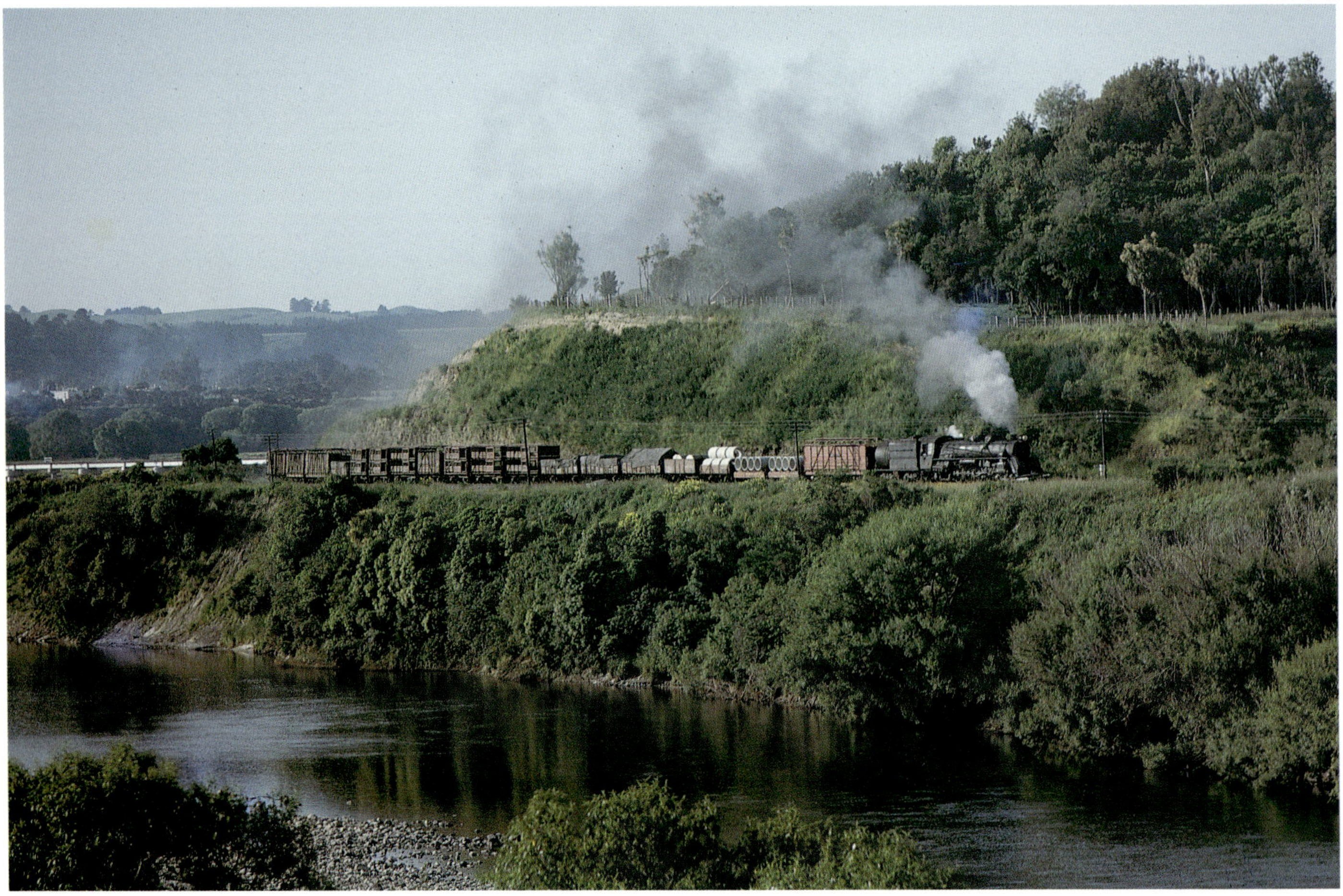

Opposite above: J 1237 heads no. 932 goods between Papatawa and Maharahara in October 1962. J.M. CREBER

Opposite below: On the approach from the west to the Manawatu Gorge, J 1238 heads no. 936 goods on 21 November 1962. The gorge is an approximately 4 km long ravine which separates the Ruahine Ranges on the northern side of the river from the Tararua Ranges on the southern side, and as such is the only gap in the dividing ranges which form a mountainous spine up the North Island from Cook Strait to the Bay of Plenty. It is also the dividing line between the southern Hawkes Bay, northern Wairarapa and northern Manawatu. J.M. CREBER

Below: KA 951 with no. 932 goods between Whakaronga and Ashhurst (approximately 15 km from Palmerston North) on 6 April 1963. J.M. CREBER

Manawatu & Wellington

Above: Until 1963 the main trunk ran through the centre of Palmerston North, a convenience for travellers but a nuisance to motorists and a source of noise pollution for businesses and shoppers. K 914 departs Palmerston North with a northbound goods train on 6 December 1958. J.M. CREBER
Below: On the same day, KA 959 departs Palmerston North with no. 229 Limited Express. J.M. CREBER

Above: Kᴀ 961 departs through the Square of Palmerston North with no. 932 goods on 4 April 1963, six months before the opening of the Milson Deviation. J.M. CREBER
Below: A 601 marks the occasion of the closure of the 31 km Foxton branch, which had its junction with the main trunk at Longburn. The train of enthusiasts is seen underway from Foxton on 18 July 1959. J.M. CREBER

Above: A classic image - an express racing along the main trunk with a KA in charge! A scene near Paraparaumu, north of Wellington, on 30 August 1959. J.M. CREBER

Below: One of the most famous features of the NZR system was the 5 km Rimutaka Incline in the Southern Wairarapa, featuring gradients of between 1 in 16 and 1 in 14, and worked by special Fell engines, acquired in the late 1870s. Here a special excursion train led by H 201, with three more of the class spread through the train, storms the gradient not far out of Cross Creek in the last weeks before closure on 29 October 1955. J.M. CREBER

Section Two
The South Island

The South Island is in many respects New Zealand's great outdoor playground, with much spectacular scenery and a low population density. In the early years of European history it was nevertheless economically more important than the North Island. Rapid settlement came about to a great extent through the gold rushes in the 1860s, first in Otago and then on the West Coast. Even though the gold soon petered out, Christchurch and Dunedin were important cities early on. The former saw New Zealand's first public railway in 1863, followed quickly by Invercargill in the "deep south".

The "Vogel Era" saw a rapid expansion of rail connections throughout the island. Christchurch and Dunedin were linked by rail in 1878, followed a few months later by Invercargill. Branch lines rapidly spread to the hinterland and brought about the development that was intended of them. Nelson was the only provincial centre not to be connected by rail to any other, although early on it did have a line to its southern hinterland, which reached 100 km before being closed in 1955.

Much of the South Island's rural-based rail network quickly lost relevance in the motorised road transport age, however. Other than a couple of preserved tourist railways and industrial spurs, only two branch lines remain in Canterbury, Otago and Southland, out of the more than 30 that once existed. From a photographic viewpoint, many of these lines had a similarity about them, and in most cases a photo of an AB hauling a mixed train on one of them could just as easily have been taken on any other. The trunk linking Christchurch, Dunedin and Invercargill did not offer much in the way of interesting scenery either (apart from the Oamaru to Dunedin section), but the Canterbury Plains made for a great "racetrack" over which J- and JA-hauled expresses (unofficially) clocked up some impressive speeds.

However, marvellous scenery was to be had on the 236 km Central Otago line from Dunedin to Cromwell, the Midland Line across the Southern Alps to the West Coast, and generally the whole of the West Coast.

In the 1960s, Westland was a mecca for steam buffs. A century before, in the 1860s, it was an economic boom region with a population swollen by the gold rush to 50,000, yet within 20 years it was dotted with derelict ghost towns and its population had halved. This state of decline never seemed to be arrested, and today it still has an atmosphere of rustic dereliction. But combined with its lush native rain forest, rugged terrain and backdrop of snow-covered alps, it was the best imaginable setting for a great variety of steam locomotive power, which in the mid-1960s still operated as if nothing had really changed for half a century or more.

Even here, however, the economies of diesels could not be ignored by the railway administrators, and by the end of the decade, steam had gone from the Coast as well. Only the South Island Main Trunk still saw regular steam-operated passenger trains with the dawning of the 1970s, and that was not for long. On 26 October 1971 came the last run of a J- and JA-hauled night limited express between Christchurch and Invercargill. Steam, officially, was over.

Marlborough & Canterbury

Above: From its completion in 1945 until the early 1960s, nearly all train haulage over the 350 km Christchurch to Picton line (or Main North Line) was handled by the ABs. Here AB 813 crosses the 293 metre long Wairau River bridge north of Blenheim on 12 October 1956. BOB HEPBURN

Below: The Main South Line heavyweights - the J series - were not allowed north of Kaikoura because of bridge weakness at Awatere and Clarence. Here JA 1247 stops at Hundalee next to the Conway River (the Marlborough/Canterbury border) with no. 65 with car goods from Christchurch on 10 January 1958. J.M. CREBER

Above: An AB with a goods train for Christchurch crosses the Waiau River south of Parnassus on 10 January 1958. J.M. CREBER

Below: The workaday world of NZR steam was not always glamorous or scenic, but on dull days the sense of power and dynamism of an express could often be heightened. At 8.40 am on 8 November 1969, a 144 express to Invercargill departs Christchurch behind JA 1248. On the right is AB 778. TONY HURST

Right: Perhaps more poignantly than any other scene, this view at Linwood Depot in May 1968 depicts the transition from steam to diesel at that time. New DJ class diesels, resplendent in their "Nippon Pink" livery, wait to displace the steamers on South Island main trunk and branch lines. In the electric shed and also from Japan, new EA electrics for the Arthur's Pass to Otira section await their transportation there. J.M. CREBER

Below: The largest purpose built steam shunter on NZR was the 2-6-2 C class from 1930, of which 24 were built. C 863 sits at Linwood Depot, Christchurch, in August 1962. It was withdrawn the following year. J.M. CREBER

Opposite below: The first line on which steam power was displaced in New Zealand also ran through Linwood, namely the 10 km Christchurch to Lyttelton line, which was electrified in 1929. EC 8 halts at Heathcote on the Christchurch side of the tunnel with a suburban train for Christchurch on 10 September 1960. The line was dieselised 10 years later. BOB HEPBURN

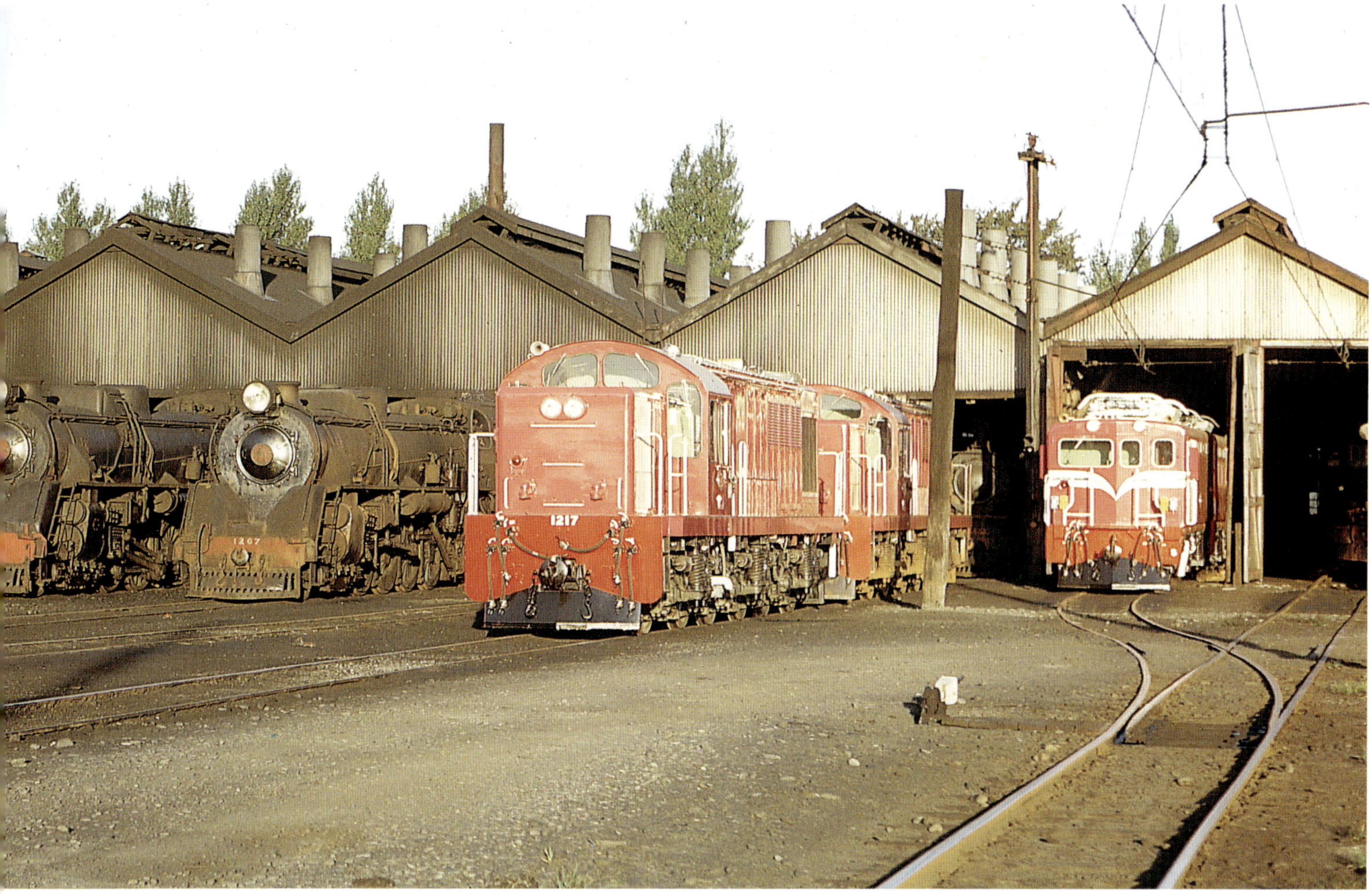
1217

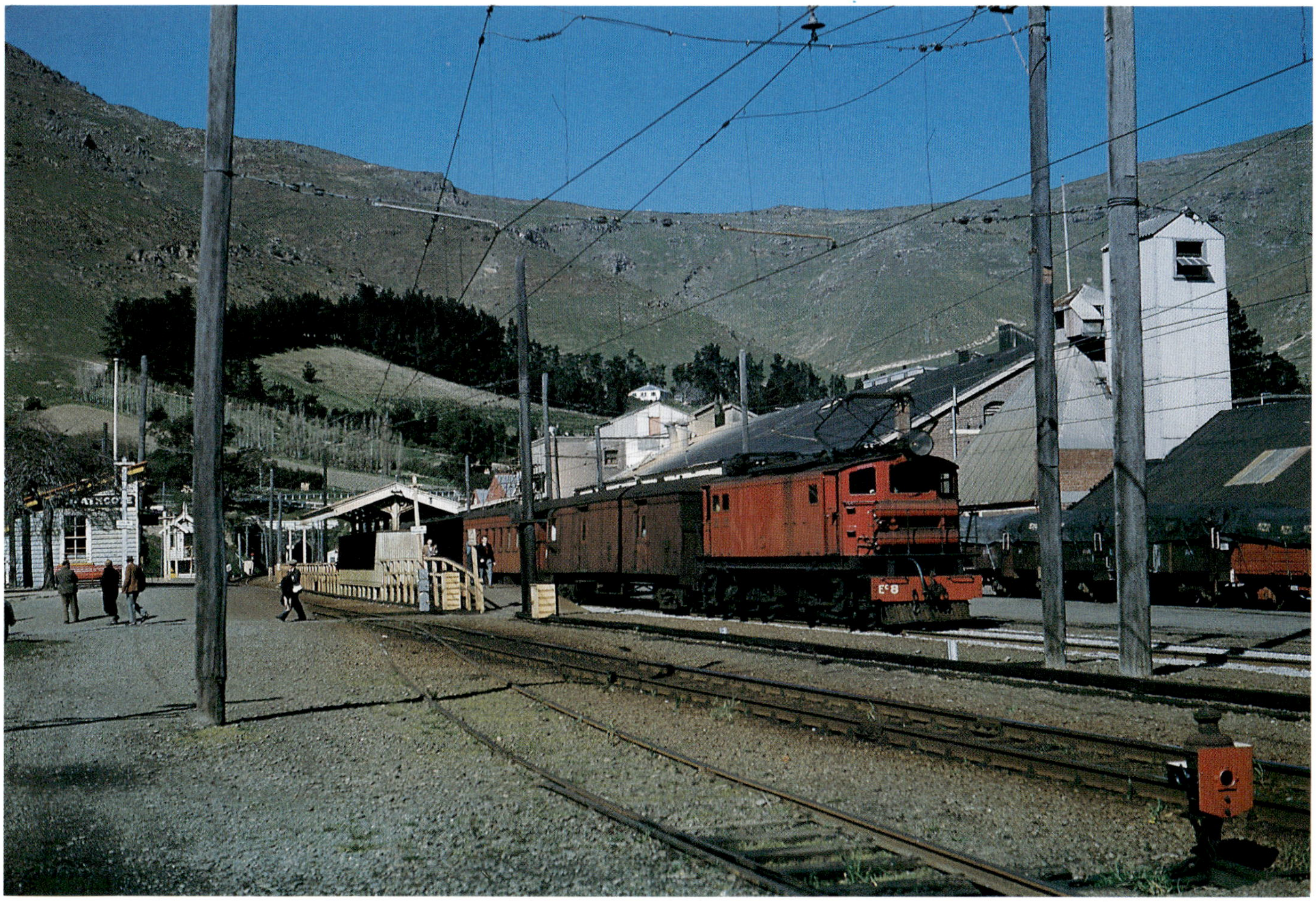

Above: The largest steam locomotives used in the South Island were the six of the 4-8-4 KB class, built for the Springfield to Arthur's Pass section of the Midland Line in 1939. Here KB 968 on no. 167 goods heads out of Christchurch on 23 March 1968. J.M. CREBER

Below: Exactly 170 km south of Christchurch is Timaru, which boasts a harbour conveniently situated close to the town. On the wharf trackage (that seen here was removed in 1960) are WF 468 and F 13 with a shuttle passenger train on 12 September 1959 at the time of the South Canterbury centennial. J.M. CREBER

Above: Also at Timaru, KB 968 departs the station area with a southbound express in March 1969.
J.M. CREBER
Below: The southernmost of the Canterbury branches, and one of the first to lose its passenger traffic, was the 7.4 km line from Studholm Junction to Waimate. A 421 sits at the terminus with no. 241 goods on 3 January 1958. BOB HEPBURN

*Above: Springfield on the Midland Line and the beginning of K*B *country! K*B *970 gets ready for its journey to Arthur's Pass with an NZRLS excursion train in September 1968. J.M. CREBER*
*Below: A K*B *heads an eastbound goods train between the Kowai River and Springfield in March 1968.*
J.M. CREBER

Above: KB 970 on no. 150 goods climbs the Otarama Bank between Staircase and Kowai Bush on 19 March 1968. J.M. CREBER
Below: KB 967 on no. 168 goods for Springfield thunders up the Cass Bank on 20 March 1968. J.M. CREBER

Above: The Cass Bank, for Canterbury rail fans at least, was the location for the best in New Zealand rail photography. Heavy coal, timber and general goods trains had to storm up the 7.5 km of 1 in 50 gradients against the backdrop of the Southern Alps. KB 970 thunders up with no. 150 goods in tow on 15 August 1962. J.M. CREBER

Below: KB 968 (the only preserved member of the KBs) is seen nearing Cass with no. 168 goods on 25 March 1968. J.M. CREBER

Above: Late on a winter evening, Ja 1267 approaches Cass (about midway along the Bank) with a snow excursion train returning to Christchurch on 25 August 1963. The former turning triangle can be seen in the foreground. J.M. CREBER

Below: Viewed from a similar vantage point, but on the other side of the track, and on a frosty winter morning, a Kb heads a loaded coal train into Cass in August 1960. PETER J. MELLOR

*Above: J*A *1257 runs along the Waimakariri River, having just crossed it further back, with no. 168 goods on 15 August 1962.* J.M. CREBER

*Below: The Waimakariri River bridge is the setting for this view taken on 12 July 1960. A K*B *with its westbound goods train is reflected in the river waters.* J.M. CREBER

Above: One of the favourite photo locations on the Midland Line is the first Bealey River bridge, not far from Arthur's Pass. Here it is crossed by KB 970 with no. 139 goods on 15 August 1962. J.M. CREBER
Below: Another well-used photo location is the Rough Creek bridge, just at the entrance to Arthur's Pass station yard. KB 965 arrives with a snow excursion train on 31 May 1959. J.M. CREBER

Westland

ABs 722 and 723 storm up the Otira River valley towards Aickens with no. 766 goods on 16 August 1962.
J.M. CREBER

Above: A 423, on its delivery run from Greymouth to its eventual resting place at Te Awamutu in the North Island, passes by Lake Brunner, the largest lake in Westland, on 29 August 1970. J.M. CREBER
Below: J 1226 on a goods for Otira seen between Stillwater and Kokiri on 5 April 1968. J.M. CREBER

Above: B 303 on no. 708 goods at Stillwater, the junction of the Midland Line and the line to Westport, on 20 August 1962. J.M. CREBER
Below: Late in the afternoon, A 474 on no. 780 mixed train departs Stillwater on 24 August 1962. J.M. CREBER

Above: UC 365 on no. 815 goods from Reefton arrives at Brunner on 21 November 1956.
J.M. CREBER

Below: J 1226 is seen passing along the bank of the Grey River between Dobson and Brunner with a goods for Otira. J.M. CREBER

Above: In March 1969, not long before the disappearance of steam from the Coast, A 602 heads a train consisting mostly of empty coal wagons across the Cobden bridge at Greymouth to the mines at Rapahoe. J.M. CREBER

Below: Just south of Greymouth, AB 704 heads a morning train to Hokitika in March 1969. J.M. CREBER

Above: At Hokitika, UC 365 sits awaiting its next turn of duty on 3 January 1958. *J.M. CREBER*
Below: The classic lines of A 475 seen on the Greymouth to Ross branch near Takutai, just south of Hokitika. The Hokitika branch still survives, but its 23 km extension south to Ross was closed in 1980. *BOB HEPBURN*
Opposite: An A is captured on film heading southwards from Greymouth towards Hokitika on 17 November 1956. *J.M. CREBER*

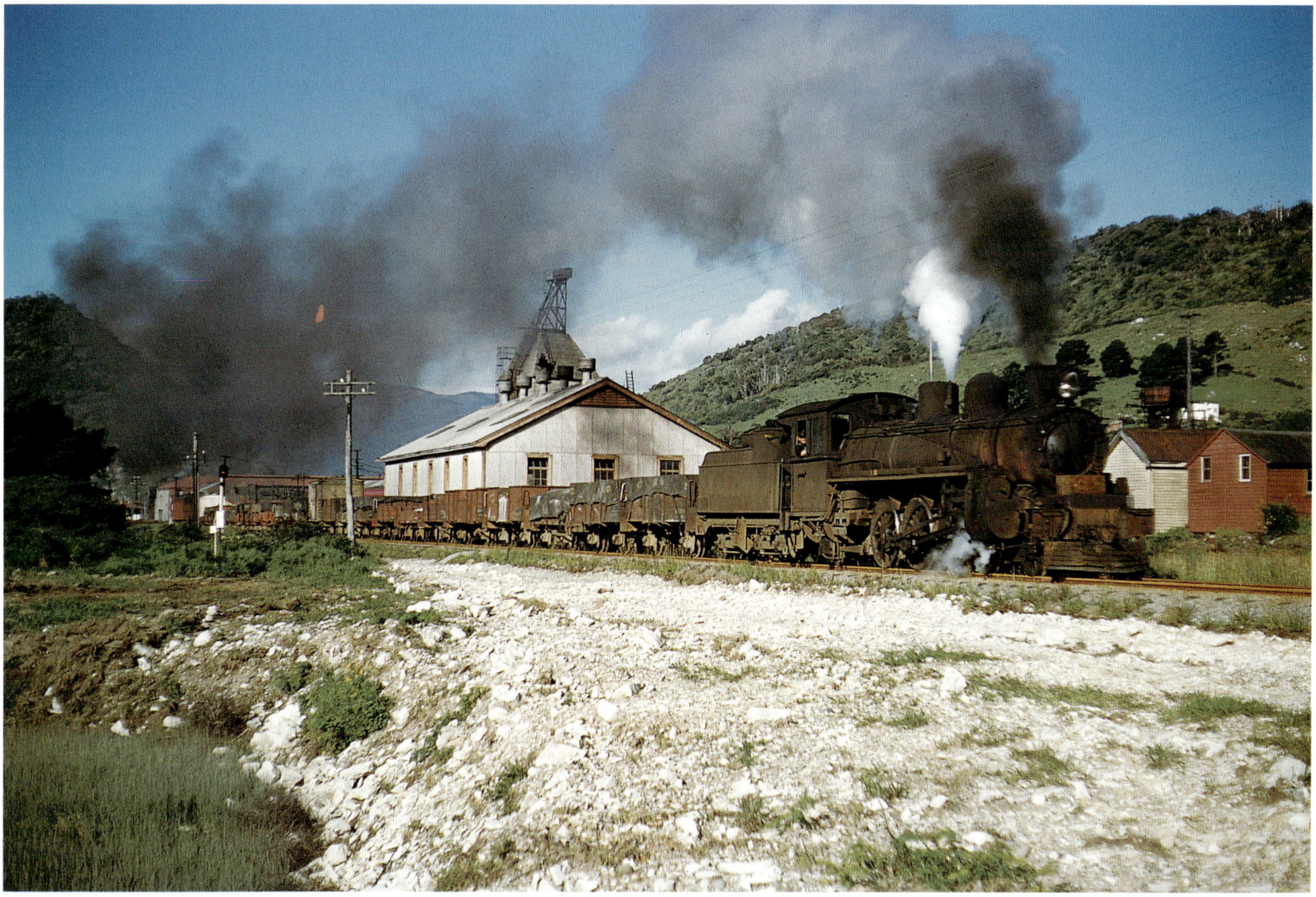

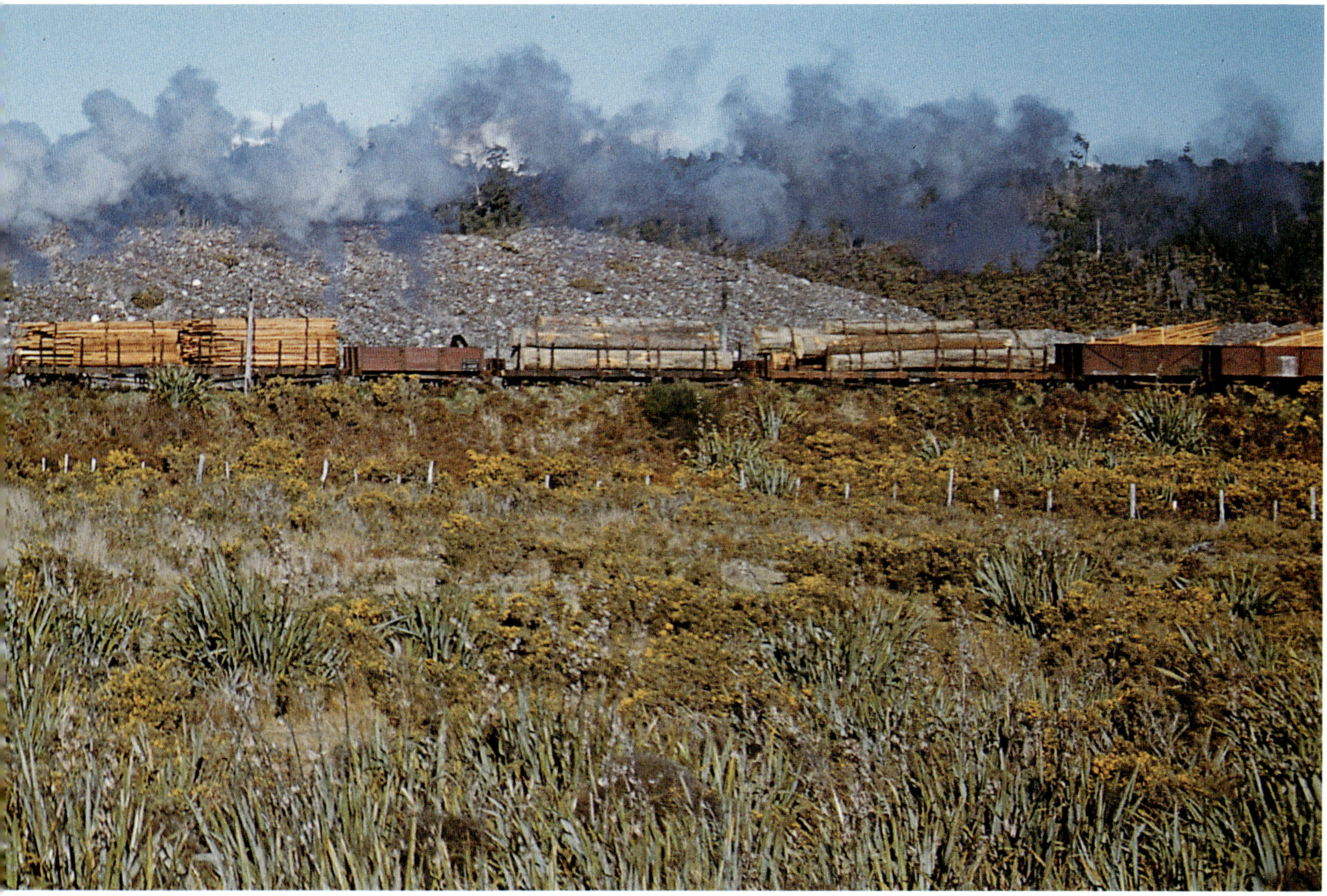

Two views of A 602 en route from Greymouth to the mines at Rapahoe in March 1969. Above: Near Camp. Below: Near Runanga. J.M. CREBER

Left: Two of the "Vogel Era" Fs, F 5 and 277 (the latter, known on the Coast as the "Hungerford F", featuring a larger cab added by a private contractor to the Greymouth Harbour Board, to whom it was at one time on loan) sit on the turntable at the Elmer Lane depot on 22 November 1956. At the end of the steam era this was a favourite haunt of rail buffs. J.M. CREBER

Above: At Runanga was a fork, the more famous of the two branches leading to Rewanaui. WE 375 leads a mixed train through Runanga in March 1969. J.M. CREBER

Right: At the next station up from Runanga, Ww 678 (in the foregound) and Ww 480 (in the distance) are seen in March 1969. These were two of three Wws converted for use on the incline in the 1960s. J.M. CREBER

Above: Under way on the incline. Between Dunollie and Rewanui, the line climbed 163 metres in 5.4 km on gradients of 1 in 26. Accordingly a Fell-type centre rail was installed to assist braking trains on the descent and was used until 1966. J.M. CREBER

Right: WE 375 (converted from B 309 in 1943) storms up the incline with an empty coal train on 28 August 1962. J.M. CREBER

Above: The first locomotive built by NZR, W 192, sits at Rewanui with no. 870 mixed train on 16 November 1956. J.M. CREBER
Below: WE 376 at Rewanui with mixed train no. 845 on 20 August 1962. J.M. CREBER

Above: WA 217 prepares to depart Ngahere with a Blackball Branch shunt on 20 November 1956. J.M. CREBER
Below: The terminus of the Blackball Branch with the same train as above. This line was to close ten years later. J.M. CREBER

Above: Between the junction with the main Westport line at Ngahere and Blackball, the Grey River had to be crosssed with a combined road / rail bridge, as well as the Firewood Creek on a timber trestle bridge. Here B 303 is seen on the latter with no. 768 goods on 20 August 1962. J M CREBER

Below: B 303 with the first half of this train at Blackball a little earlier (the gradient and weight restrictions required splitting some trains in two). J M CREBER

Above: Wa 217 heads up the 1 in 25 incline to Roa, 2.7 km further on from Blackball, on 20 November 1956. This section was owned by the Mines Department from September 1909 until closure on 27 July 1960. Because of the gradient, this line used a Fell-type centre rail for braking trains on the way down. Only the brake van is being taken up in this scene. J.M. CREBER

Below: A little later, Wa 289 descends the Roa incline with wagons laden with coal. The coal was brought to the railhead via cable inclines. Roa was on the other side of the Paparoa Range from Rewanui, and some coal came from the same seams as those at Rewanui. J.M. CREBER

Above: In the second earliest scene in this book, B 303, with UC 370 banking, moves a Greymouth-bound goods train up the Reefton saddle on 18 November 1955. J.M. CREBER
Below: South of Reefton, B 306 moves train 777 with BA 149 pushing at the train end on 20 August 1959. BOB HEPBURN

Another Reefton Saddle scene: A 428 on no. 819 goods, with A 418 banking at the rear, not far from the Tawhai Tunnel on 24 August 1962. J.M. CREBER

Above: At Reefton, B 307 crosses BA *148 on 14 November 1956. J.M. CREBER*
Below: Between Waitahu and Reefton, A 423 heads no. 775 goods southbound on 3 January 1958.
J.M. CREBER

Above: At the end of the 2.9 km Conns Creek Branch was another famous feature of the West Coast, the Denniston Incline. This was a self-acting (gravity fed) cable incline which rose 584 metres to reach the coal mines at Denniston and was as steep as 1 in 1.25 at one point. This view, taken on top of a descending loaded coal wagon, looks down at Conns Creek, with the steam plume of WW 680 visible. J.M. CREBER
Below: A close-up view of WW 680, visible in the photo above. This is March 1967. Five months later, on 6 August, the incline and the branch passed into history. J.M. CREBER

Above: North of Westport on the then Seddonville Branch (now Ngakawau Branch), Ww 684 heads a goods southbound to Westport on 8 January 1958, seen here at Waimangaroa, the junction for the Conns Creek Branch. The Conns Creek Branch can be seen heading off to the right. J.M. CREBER

Below: With evidence of track subsidence caused by the magnitude 7 Inangahua earthquake of 24 May 1968, an AB heads a goods train southwards from Inangahua in June of that year. J.M. CREBER

Opposite: To get its train on to the combined road/rail bridge north of Landing, southbound A 428 has to climb a gradient caused by track subsidence. J.M. CREBER

Otago

At Dunedin's fine George Troup designed railway station in March 1964, a JA arrives with an express to Invercargill, while AB 746 waits to depart with a suburban passenger train to Mosgiel. J.M. CREBER

Right: F 12, Yorkshire builders no. 241, was built in 1874, and in 1957 was sold to the Waitaki Farmers Freezing Company in Pukeuri. In 1968 it was obtained by the NZRLS, the Otago Branch taking the cab for use on its Ocean Beach Railway, and the Canterbury Branch taking the rest, which is now stored at Ferrymead Historic Park. This photo was taken in 1960.
PETER J. MELLOR

Above: Pukeuri was also the junction for the 59 km branch to Kurow, at the end of which AB 788 is seen with a goods train on 8 September 1960. This branch survived until 1983.
BOB HEPBURN

Right: D 6, originally an NZR engine, seen at the McDonald's Limeworks, by whom it was purchased from the Taratu Coal Company in 1940, at Whitecraig near Oamaru in 1960. It was donated to the Ocean Beach Railway in Dunedin in 1965.
PETER J. MELLOR

Above: A southbound "South Island Limited" travels along the coastline near Shag Point in 1966.
Below: JA 1250 (now preserved) heads no. 310 goods between Puketeraki and Merton on 11 October 1966.
J.M. CREBER

Above: JA 1260 heads south through Warrington with no. 143 Limited Express on 11 March 1968.
Below: With Blueskin Bay in the background, JA 1261 with a northbound Limited Express in March 1968.
J.M. CREBER

Above: JA 1259 with no. 144 northbound express heads past the junction with the Port Chalmers Branch at Sawyers Bay on 11 October 1966. Despite the upgrade, good smoke effects were the exception at this location. J.M. CREBER

Below: AB 608 heads out of Dunedin station with no. 344 suburban passenger train from Dunedin to Port Chalmers on 6 March 1964. For a while this loco was stored at Ferrymead Historic Park. J.M. CREBER

Above: On 6 March 1964, AB 608 (now being restored in the North Island) departs Maia with no. 344 suburban train to Port Chalmers. Below: The same service with AB 658 crosses the causeway near St Leonards in October 1966. J.M CREBER

*Above: JA 1254 on no. 387 goods for Invercargill near Dunedin on 13 October 1966. J.M. CREBER
Below: Between Kensington and Caversham in Dunedin's southern suburbs, a JA is seen heading an
Invercargill-bound express on 14 March 1964. J.M. CREBER*

Right: AB 782 has emerged from the Chain Hills tunnel with its subbie to Mosgiel, and now approaches Wingatui, the junction for the branch to Otago Central, on 14 March 1964.
J.M. CREBER

Below: The furthest the Otago Central Railway reached was Cromwell, 236 km from Wingatui. A panorama of the terminus station and yard, with the town in the distance, taken on 10 January 1958.
BOB HEPBURN

Above: Four days earlier, on 6 January 1958, AB 793 was photographed with train no. 364 in the Cromwell Gorge. With the development of the hydro power dam at Clyde, the gorge was flooded in 1992, and the road now takes a course high on the hillside. The railway disappeared in 1980. BOB HEPBURN

Below: At Lauder, 65 km from Cromwell, AB 779 sits with no. 439 goods for Cromwell on 10 January 1958. BOB HEPBURN

AB 812 with no. 411 goods for Cromwell on 9 January 1958, seen at a place known as Hartley's Beach.
BOB HEPBURN

Above: In its last two months of life, the northbound "South Island Limited" is seen south of Mosgiel with JA *1261 in front in September 1970.* J.M. CREBER
Below: The same train seen earlier, heading past Lake Waihola. J.M. CREBER

Above: Just south of Balclutha was the junction for the 68 km Catlins River Branch (also known as the Tahakopa Branch), which had connections from several sawmilling lines over its most southerly sections. A 478 is seen at Owaka, about halfway along the line, with no. 486 passenger train on 14 January 1958. Passenger services ended in December of that year, although the line itself survived until 27 February 1971. BOB HEPBURN

Below: An NZRLS excursion with AB 717 on the Catlins River Branch on 7 March 1964. J.M. CREBER

Although late September 1970, snow covers the ground in this scene of a northbound South Island Limited, headed by JA 1258. J.M. CREBER

Above: The second longest branch line in Otago was the 94 km Roxburgh Branch from Milton. On 19 October 1966, AB 694 heads a general goods train near Lawrence. J.M. CREBER
Below: On the same day, AB 794 heads a train of "super" between Waitahuna and Lawrence. J.M. CREBER

Southland

Above: The first branch line encountered in Southland when heading south on the main trunk was the 42 km line north from Waipahi, known as the Tapanui Branch, although it actually went beyond that locality as far as Edievale until 1968. The section through Tapanui to Heriot lasted until 1978. A 411 with no. 514 goods on 6 January 1958. BOB HEPBURN

Below: The next branch along was the 21 km from McNab to Waikaka, which, like many lines, was closed in early 1962 when there was no longer any restriction on the transport of livestock by road. A 406 with no. 427 goods at the terminus on 13 January 1958. BOB HEPBURN

Above: The 59 km Waimea Plains line from Gore to Lumsden was built to provide a quick access to central southland from Dunedin. Most of it was closed in 1971, although part of it from Lumsden to Belfour lasted until January 1978. A 427 with a goods train on 9 January 1958. BOB HEPBURN
Below: North of Lumsden on the Kingston Branch, AB 729 is seen with a goods train for Kingston on 9 January 1958, the Oreti River forming a backdrop. BOB HEPBURN

Above: A world of blue and white is the setting as southbound AB 726 heads through a snow-covered landcsape on no. 668 goods after departing Kingston on 26 July 1960. In the background is Lake Wakatipu. J.M. CREBER

Below: The 24 km branch from Invercargill to Bluff is, naturally, the most southerly in the country. A 161 and WF 844 head no. 543 goods through flat landscape on 7 January 1958. BOB HEPBURN

An image like this one serves as a fitting farewell: with exhausts roaring and flanges squealing, KA 942 and KA 934 attack the 1 in 50 gradient out of Raurimu and up the Spiral in July 1964. PETER J. MELLOR

Further reading

Steam locomotives and their operation on the New Zealand Government Railways system have been the subject of a comprehensive literature over the years, of which the best is listed below. Information on steam locomotives used by private industry, on the other hand, is scarce. Some will be found in *New Zealand Locomotives and Railcars 1992* and *New Zealand Steam Locomotives by Official Number*.

G.B. Churchman, *New Zealand Locomotives and Railcars 1992*, IPL Books, 1992
G.B. Churchman & Tony Hurst, *The Railways of New Zealand: A journey through history*, HarperCollins Publishers, 1990
J. Cooke & J. Vogel, *New Zealand Steam Finale*, Collins Publishers, 1979
T.A. McGavin, *Steam Locomotives of New Zealand, Part One*, NZRLS, 1987
E.J. McClare, *Steam Locomotives of New Zealand, Part Two*, NZRLS, 1990
E.J. McClare, *Steam Locomotives of New Zealand, Part Three*, NZRLS, 1991
G. Petrie, *New Zealand Steam Locomotives by Official Number*, Locomotive Press, 1993
D.L.A. Turner, *The Last Decade*, Whitcoulls, 1977
W.W. Stewart & P.J. Mellor, *When Steam Was King*, A.H. & A.W. Reed, 1970